MENACHEM & FRED

MENACHEM & FRED

MENACHEM & FRED

Thoughts and Memories of Two Brothers

Frederick Raymes (Manfred Mayer)
Menachem (Heinz) Mayer

Translated from the Hebrew by Shulamit Berman

AMBERLEY YAD VASHEM

Language Editor: Alifa Saadya
Production Editor: Gayle Green

© First published in Hebrew 2001 and in English 2002 by Yad Vashem
This edition published 2016

Amberley Publishing
The Hill, Stroud
Gloucestershire, GL5 4EP

www.amberley-books.com

British Library Cataloguing in Publication Data.
A catalogue record for this book is available from the British Library.

ISBN 978 1 4456 5879 7 (print)
ISBN 978 1 4456 5880 3 (ebook)

Typeset in 10pt on 12pt Sabon.
Typesetting and Origination by Amberley Publishing.
Printed in the UK.

For I am the bud and the fruit
I am my future and my past
I am the barren stem
And you are my time and my song
                                        Leah Goldberg

"What more can I write?"
From a letter written by Father, Rivesaltes Camp, France, April 1941

"Are the trees in bloom over there? There are no trees here."
From a letter written by Mother, Rivesaltes Camp, France, April 20, 1941

"I don't know where we're going.
We don't in the least regret leaving you behind.
You are safer where you are."
From a letter written by Father a few days before being sent to Auschwitz, August 10, 1942

Contents

Contents

Foreword

We considered writing a joint biography. Although for the first few years a part of our lives was spent together, we experienced each event in our own way and at some point our lives diverged; perhaps it would be more accurate to say that we were separated from one another. For this reason sections of the book are presented in different styles – we begin with a dialogue and continue with a monologue, each one describing the events of his life in chronological order. We also felt it necessary to add explanatory notes – historical footnotes and general descriptions – both to enhance the reader's understanding of the subject, and to convey something of what we personally felt to be important in the chronicle of events.

Our readers are no doubt familiar with the subject of the Holocaust from school, from books, and from the media. So why do we feel it necessary to expand on the topic beyond our personal memories? First, because these events and our response to them have shaped our lives and our worldview. Second, because antisemitism and intolerance of others are still prevalent. Innocent people are still being killed out of bigotry and hatred of what is foreign or different, or because of religious differences. This destructive intolerance has been the driving force behind many events in the twentieth century.

As we enter the twenty-first century, it would seem that humanity is less civilized than ever. Murderer-statesmen continue to perpetrate evil because the nations of the world refrain from intervening in the "internal affairs" of other nations.

The international community does not interfere until it is too late, followed by a great outcry – probably to assuage an uncomfortable and oppressive sense of guilt. We feel a deep need to prevent these iniquities insofar as we are able. And perhaps one way to do so is to speak of the past.

Letters

Dear Dad and Fred,

Everyone has some things they take for granted.

But for you, life isn't something you can take for granted.
Neither are parents.

We, on the other hand –

We take life for granted

And our parents have always been there for us.

But we never had grandparents on our father's side.

For the first few years, they simply weren't there. They were
never mentioned. Nobody ever spoke about them or the fate
that befell them.

The years passed – we needed to grow, and Daddy needed to
distance himself in time from those appalling events in order to
begin telling us, slowly, haltingly, what happened to him and to
his family.

When we heard the stories, each of us tried to imagine our
grandparents: Who were they? What did they look like? How
would they look if they were with us today? What kind of
grandparents would they have been?

Now we are adults. We have children of our own. When we
re-read the letters your parents wrote in the concentration camps,
we see a different picture – we see a family. When they wrote
those letters they were approximately the same age as we are now.

The earliest letters contain striking descriptions of nature and scenery. They transmitted their love of nature to their children and grandchildren, and some of their great grandchildren have inherited it as well.

They wrote of their memories, their everyday struggles in the camps. They expressed their love for their children, their concern for their welfare and education. Above all, they conveyed their fears for the physical safety of their sons.

Despite their ever worsening situation, they continued to write to their children.

Now that we are parents ourselves, it is very difficult for us to imagine the strength of character needed for a mother to write a farewell letter to her small children. She wrote to them when she was about to board a train to Auschwitz, keenly aware that her children's lives were also in danger. She wrote to them in the full knowledge that she would never see them again.

It's true that we never knew our grandfather and grandmother, but through your stories, and especially through this book, they have become real to us. We have learned to know them a little better. We're proud to see that we and our children have inherited some of their qualities.

Thank you for giving us the opportunity to discover our roots. You have given us cause to take pride in our past. You have taught us to value and appreciate our lives – we cannot simply take them for granted.

May we learn, through you, to value life, our children, our parents, and our grandfather and grandmother.

With love,
Jonathan Michal and Zvi

Dear Dad,

When I first read the manuscript for your half of the book I was awestruck. Who was this man that was recording these memoirs and why had he not let us see him before? As I continued to read, I discovered that this man was an amazing testament to determination and spirit, something that I hope to mirror some day.

Your story let us see you, understand your nightmares, and finally figure out where some of your "quirks" come from, like your passion for "potato soup" and why you never learned to swim. It also, for the first time, gave us a glimpse of the people from whom David and I came, including our grandparents, Karl and Mathilde, and especially our mom when she was young, vivacious and well. For the first time we were exposed to your other life. Oh, we had heard bits and pieces of your life's journey but we had never been allowed to see or even get a chance to experience your pain, frustrations, losses and successes until now, until your book.

I remember the first time you came and spoke at my school. I was as mesmerized as my students. This man in the front of the room was so courageous. This guy was my Dad. That first time you spoke to a classroom packed with kids I was so proud of you. I still am. Every time you share your story you are teaching, you are a role model and you are teaching young people to never give up.

Dave and I are so grateful that you have painstakingly put your story to paper. Now not only can your family know its true history and treasure it, but the world can also have one more eyewitness account of a time in history that we, as human beings, must never forget.

Thanks Dad, without you Dave and I and all of your beautiful grandchildren would not be here today. Without this book we would still not know too much about our father or especially about his remarkable life.

We love you very much,
Suzie and David

Two Voices

Fred: In December 1946, as the harsh sound of the ship's whistle blared across the bay, the *Ile de France* docked in New York Harbor. A young man, barely seventeen years old, stood on deck, curiously observing the ship's maneuvers and gazing at the sights of New York unfolding before his eyes. There were thousands of travelers on the ship. The young man spoke French with a faint German accent. He did not speak English. He did not know a soul in America.

As he disembarked, the fact that he was alone and penniless did not particularly bother him. On the contrary, he was serenely optimistic, knowing that at last he had reached the land of opportunity.

He had survived the events of the last seven years, enduring the inferno of Europe, the Second World War, and the Holocaust. He arrived in America by himself, because only he and his small brother had survived. The younger boy remained behind, in Europe. Father, mother, grandmother, uncles, aunts, and cousins – all had perished, murdered, in the gas chambers of Auschwitz.

Who was this penniless teenage refugee? This was Manfred (Fred). Why did I come to the United States? Why did I change my name? How did I manage to get a university education despite my impossible financial situation? How did I come to be involved for forty years in the defense industry and space programs of the United States? How did I feel when I was sent by the U.S. Army to work with the German rocket expert, Werner von Braun?[1] How did I react when I visited Germany thirty-two years after deportation? Why did I wait twenty-six years to see my brother again? Why did my brother go to Israel while I went to the United States? What was it that drove us to visit Auschwitz together? Why do I still do battle with God?

I hope to answer all these questions, so that you, the children, grandchildren, and the post-World War II generation will better understand how intolerance, hatred, and world indifference can lead to catastrophic events.

Menachem: For nearly thirty-five years, I kept the past at bay. I fled from it and forgot it. Some years ago, my children and grandchildren began asking me about the past and my family. "You never told us about it!" they said. In truth, I was not in the least aware of my silence. When I looked at my grandchildren, seven and eight years old, I asked myself: "Was I really so small the last time I saw my parents?" Yet I never had these thoughts when my own children were the same age. Yes, I suppressed everything.

From that day, the idea of writing my memories took root, but it only matured in the past year. More than thirty years elapsed before I could begin peering into my past. It is dangerous to look back. It conjures up the image of Lot's wife fleeing from Sodom, the city with which she was inextricably bound: "And Lot's wife looked behind and turned into a pillar of salt" (Genesis 19:26).

The past was like a huge puzzle with many pieces missing. Slowly I put together details from libraries, archives, books, and letters. I also talked with others who had shared my fate and with people who were involved in these events, whether willingly

---

1   Werner von Braun (1912–1977) was a German scientist who worked for the Nazis during the war. He was in charge of the German rocket site at Peenemunde that developed the V-2 rocket, which rained destruction on Britain. After the Second World War, von Braun was transferred to the United States Army where he held key positions in missile development and space research.

or against their will. Some of those with whom I spoke should have remembered but preferred to forget; they were living proof of selective memory! I also attempted to gather and organize the shards of my personal recollections, those flashes that flickered in my own "black hole."

The passing of time is like the flow of water. Memories are erased over the course of time like water wearing away the stones in a riverbed. Memory and imagination are close neighbors. Memory is a relative of truth but not its twin, so it is important to document and preserve testimony. When my brother Fred and I met in September 1998 we talked about jointly writing down our memories and our personal stories of the Holocaust, about the years that preceded it and those that came after. Our target audience was our children and grandchildren, who stood before us. We decided to touch briefly on the historical and political background of the period, in an attempt to explain the inexplicable, the maelstrom of events in which we were helplessly caught. We also hoped to make it easier for the reader to make the connection between our personal stories and the historical events to which we refer.

I would like to thank all those who encouraged me to write and those who helped us collect documents and testimonies.

First of all, to my children, who urged me to put these memories down on paper, and the older grandchildren who asked questions about the past.

To Jacqueline Sallebert and Nelly Lemaire, who were in charge of the children in Aspet orphanage, I love you both.

To the pastor of Hoffenheim, Rev. Matthias Uhlig, who sought in his own way to atone for the Nazi deeds, and who asked me, in vain, to bridge the distance between Jerusalem and the village of my birth, Hoffenheim.[2]

---

2   I turned down his request, explaining that a bridge needs to be supported from both ends, while it seems to me that this bridge has only one support – Jerusalem. As far as I am concerned, Hoffenheim is a void!

To Pastor Ludwig Streib of Hoffenheim, who, when studying at the seminary, wrote a thesis about the Jewish community. He provided us with a vast amount of material, some forgotten, in some cases never known, about life in this remote village, about our family and even about us, the children.

And last but definitely not least, to Rev. Albrecht Lohrbacher, a man of the cloth and an educator, and his wife Ulrike, righteous Christians both, who helped and encouraged me from the outset.

I also want to thank all those who read the manuscript and offered their suggestions: my companion Uri Landau; Nitza Shachal, for her interest and involvement; my friend Dr. Yehezkel Cohen, for his wise and perceptive remarks; Naora Yahav who assisted with the editing. My thanks also go to Yad Vashem for publishing the book.

PART I

Together

Early Memories

We were born in the small village of Hoffenheim in Baden, southwest Germany, near where the Neckar river flows into the Rhine, some twenty-five kilometers from the university town of Heidelberg. The village nestles among verdant fields and woodland. Everything is leafy and green. It is hard to believe that the events that occurred in these beautiful and pastoral surroundings were so horrifying that they changed our lives beyond recognition.

Actually, it's not so surprising. More than one thousand years ago, during the Crusades, Jewish blood was shed when the inhabitants of the Rhine area attacked local communities. In later years, Jews were accused of murdering Christians for ritual purposes, such as using Christian children to make matsos for Passover. These outrageous stories could be heard as late as the twentieth century. Clearly, the difference between then and now is that those were the "dark Middle Ages"; we, after all, lived in the rational, scientific, cultured, and enlightened twentieth century…

In 1720, there were six Jewish families in Hoffenheim. They were forced to pay the feudal authorities for protection – a special tax imposed on the Jews that gave them the right to live in the village. That year each family paid six gulden. By the mid-nineteenth century the community had grown to 227, comprising fifteen percent of the total population of the village.

In the eighteenth century the Jews of Hoffenheim earned their living as cattle traders, farmers, and moneylenders. This last occupation fueled the simmering embers of antisemitism, because non-Jews vented their anger on those who lent them money to repay their debts, rather than on the authorities who could imprison them until their debts were paid. Some two hundred years later, the Nazis applied a similar system of "lawful" robbery on a far greater scale!

At the end of the nineteenth century there were forty-eight Jewish families in the village – cattle traders, shopkeepers, tradesmen, merchants, and others. When civil rights were granted (Emancipation) in the early 1800s and people began to move to the cities, many Jews, including those of Hoffenheim, relocated to larger towns. At the beginning of the twentieth century there were still one hundred and seventeen Jews in the village, but the community was shrinking; by the early 1930s only forty remained – 2.8 percent of the population.

The synagogue was built in the mid-eighteenth century. It stood in the Neuestrasse, near the center of the village. Despite the small size of the community and the fact that there was no rabbi, services and events were held regularly until November 10, 1938, when the building was destroyed during Kristallnacht. Before that, in 1933, it was decided that all the religious needs of the village would be provided by the regional rabbinate in nearby Sinsheim. Apart from the synagogue, Hoffenheim had a mikve (ritual bath), separate burial societies for men and for women, a fund to aid the sick, and a synagogue building fund.

In 1840 a Jewish school had been opened in Hoffenheim. It had continued to function until 1876, when the local Catholic, Protestant, and Jewish schools merged. From the beginning of the twentieth century until 1937, religious instruction was taught in the synagogue.

In 1933, the total population of Hoffenheim numbered 1,440. The majority were farmers, but there were also a few tradesmen and laborers. This was typical of the villages in the northern region of Baden. Some 86 percent of the population was Protestant, 11 percent were Catholics, and Jews made up less than 3 percent.

Fred: Our parents married in 1927. Father was thirty-three; Mother was twenty-nine. They were not particularly well off. I assume it was an arranged marriage, as was customary in those days, and mother's dowry played a significant role in making the match.

Mother's name was Mathilde, but she was known as Hilde. Her maiden name was Wertheimer. She was born on June 8, 1898, in Neidenstein, a village not far from Hoffenheim. Her mother, our grandmother Mina, and her brother Emanuel continued to live there.

Father's name was Karl. He came from a family of tailors. He had a brother named Moritz, the father of Ingrid (who now lives in California), and a sister named Elsa. Aunt Elsa never married, but in 1920 she gave birth to a son, whose father was a non-Jewish neighbor. This twofold disgrace must have caused a huge scandal at the time. It was only in the 1960s that I heard the story for the first time, when Aunt Elsa came to visit me in California. Following family tradition, Elsa was also a seamstress. She managed to emigrate to England at the very last minute, in 1939.

As far as I know, Father's schooling was limited to the elementary level. I don't know where he attended school. He was born in Frankfurt-am-Main on September 29, 1894. His parents moved to Hoffenheim when he was two years old. At some point, my father was apprenticed to his uncle, the proprietor of Heumann's Kosher Butchery. This is the Heumann with whom we lived after Kristallnacht, the brother of the man who provided me with an affidavit to come to the United States after the war.

When the First World War broke out in 1914, Father was drafted into the German Kaiser's army. He was twenty years old, and entered the army as a private, but in time he was promoted to the rank of corporal. In 1917, he was apparently captured by British forces. At the end of the war, he was decorated with the Iron Cross.[3] The Kaiser welcomed all "cannon fodder" with open arms, Jews and non-Jews alike. Most German Jews were deeply

---

3 This medal of distinction was first awarded to Prussian heroes in 1813 during the Napoleonic wars. Recipients included soldiers who distinguished themselves in the Franco-Prussian War of 1870 and those who displayed outstanding courage in the First World War. Hitler continued the tradition, bestowing the Iron Cross during the Second World War.

patriotic in spite of a long history of persecution, discrimination, and antisemitism. To a certain degree, Jewish veterans who had served in the army were somewhat protected, even during Hitler's regime – but this didn't last!

I know very few details about my birth, but I remember stories about how cold it was during that February in 1929 – they said it was so cold that the River Rhine froze and you could walk from one side to the other on the ice.

My mother gave birth to me at home, as was customary at the time. I assume there was a midwife but no doctor. Mother gave me a very Germanic name – Manfred. When I asked why she chose that name, she replied that it was very popular. When she was young she heard a neighbor calling her son from the window… Manfred. She liked the sound.

Frequently on Saturdays we visited our grandmother Mina whom we called Oma, German for Grandma. All four of us went to visit her – Father, Mother, my three-year-old brother Heinz, and I. The path was endless for young legs. It led through fields and forests to Neidenstein, my mother's birthplace, a few kilometers from Hoffenheim.

Menachem: I remember those walks through the forest. I also remember how frightened I was of the ghosts and spirits that are so typical of German folklore. When I was born they named me Heinz, or Heinzl. My mother revealed that my Jewish name was Menachem in a letter that she wrote around the time of my older brother's bar mitzvah, which took place in a Toulouse cellar in 1942.

Fred: Many years later, I realized that Oma was really our step-grandmother; our mother's birth-mother died before we were born and her father (grandfather Maier) remarried. He also died before we were born. I received my Hebrew name in his memory.

I remember Mother had very long brown hair, which she gathered up in a bun. I think she was better educated than father.

She played the zither, a stringed instrument similar to a small harp. I know very little about her parents.

Menachem: While searching for papers and documentation I came across a file on our family in the city of Karlsruhe archives. It included questionnaires for issuing identity documents and provided details about us all. Mother's father, Maier Wertheimer – for whom Manfred is named – owned a shoe business. The name of our biological grandmother was Hanchen, or Hannah, née Kaufmann. The documents also revealed that our parents were married on November 6, 1927, in the village of Neidenstein.

Photographs of Father, Mother and Fred were attached to the documents. The pictures had been taken at the same time that the questionnaires were filled in, which would have been at the end of 1938 or early in 1939. I had forgotten my parents' faces, but when I saw the pictures I remembered instantly. It was quite obvious from the photo that my father had recently returned from Dachau concentration camp.

We called our parents Vater and Mutter (Father and Mother) as was customary at the time. I am quite certain we had a sheltered childhood. Our relationship with our parents was warm and loving. We had a good childhood, paradoxical as it sounds in light of the events that befell us, and our parents protected us as best they could from the outside world.

I have often been asked: "How do you explain the fact that you remained emotionally healthy, after all that you and your brother lived through?" I think it's because our early years were happy, those years that are crucial for the stable, confident, and secure development of the child. Children are by nature egocentric. If the nuclear family is strong, nurturing, and protective, then nothing can harm them.

Fred: Oma had a son named Emanuel who was Mother's step-brother. His name means "God is with us" in Hebrew, and it's hard not to wonder how much his name helped him, and indeed to what extent God was with him. Emanuel was forty years old when he was killed in the gas chambers at Auschwitz. We loved visiting our grandmother and Uncle Emanuel. He had a car! Every day he drove to work in the town of Bruchsal, until they moved there in 1936. In those days it was no small matter to own a car!

In the early 1930s, the routine of our family life remained almost unvaried. We children were protected from the horrendous events taking place outside of our world. Hitler had come to power in 1933. I was four, Menachem one year old. Up until 1935, things were reasonably quiet in our somewhat isolated village. In the large cities, particularly Berlin, anti-Jewish activity was much more strident.

I remember going for walks on Saturday with Father in the woods near Hoffenheim. We would stop at the bakery to buy a warm pretzel, fresh from the oven. They were large, crisp and salty, a real Sabbath treat. I can still hear the call of the cuckoo echoing through the woods as we ambled along. Thirty-two years later, when I returned to Germany, I was drawn to those woods as iron filings to a magnet.

Menachem: I had a remarkably similar experience. When I returned to Germany for the first time in 1974, I went to the woods, and something tugged at my heart. The colors and smells were so familiar, as if it was only yesterday that I left – and I was filled with longing for a world that is no more.

Fred: I remember Father's stories about the First World War. In particular, I remember his reply to my repeated questions about why he was bald and his head was as smooth as an egg! He told me that once, during the war, he and his comrades were sent to carry out a mission on a very hot day. Later, when his unit came to the trough to water the horses, the soldiers plunged their heads in the water to cool off – his hair fell out and never grew back again. For some reason this story, told on a cold winter day, the family cozily together, reminds me of Mother playing on the zither and singing the famous German song, Lorelei, about a large rock in the River Rhine said to be haunted by a beautiful maiden who lures sailors to their destruction with her song.

Menachem: I remember sitting on Father's lap on the Sabbath while he told me stories. It was in the service apartment adjoining the synagogue, where we lived until it was destroyed together with the synagogue on Kristallnacht in 1938. I must have been four or five years old. I particularly remember a story about a terribly cold winter, when the soldiers emerged from the trenches to relieve themselves: "It was so cold that when we peed it froze in mid-flow." This tale evidently made a strong impression on me, because I still remember it.

Fred: When the weather made it impossible to go out, we played in the attic. In those days there were no shopping centers or supermarkets, so all kinds of food products were stored up there. Mother used to dry apple slices in late summer. When the sun heated the tiles on the roof, the space underneath grew warm and the whole house was filled with the pungent aroma of ripe apples. In the springtime, before Passover, large bundles of round matzos were stored up there a short time before the festival. I guess the mice had a real party! A whole collection of other objects was piled in one corner of the attic. We didn't know what they were. Among them were some holy books, old and tattered, that were destined for the geniza (ritual burial), because holy books are never burned or thrown out. Other creepy things for kids like the straps used for lowering coffins into graves were stored there... Each Jewish community had its own burial society, which performed the duties of today's undertaker. This was considered the most meritorious good deed an individual could perform.

That reminds me of the time Uncle Emanuel drove us to the local Jewish cemetery, deep in the forest near the town of Waibstadt. According to Jewish custom, family members visit

the graves of their family every year, before the high holidays.
I remember how we children sat in the car and waited for the
adults, wondering what they were doing over there on the other
side of the fence... Children were not allowed into the cemetery
while their parents were alive. Everything appeared shrouded in
mystery. The sighing of the wind in the dense forest, the rustling
of pinecones and dry leaves under the wheels of the car as it
slowly climbed the hill, filled us with dread. Thirty-two years
later, in 1972, I returned to that place, seeking my roots.

The family's financial situation was not good; in fact you could
say we were poor. Our grandmother and Uncle Emanuel, who
was at the time a senior employee in a plant that built stoves,
were better off, so on our visits to them we often came away
with new clothes. I still remember my first suit – it was green.
But what impressed me most was the inner pocket, containing a
tiny mirror, a small pencil and a notebook.

Uncle Emanuel never forgot our birthdays. His present to us
was always the same – a large five-mark coin. I don't know what
could be bought with it; we never got to spend it, because it went
straight into our moneybox.

I remember another visit in 1939 to Oma in Bruchsal. The war
had broken out by then and suddenly we heard bombs falling.
One of them fell close to the window of the room in which I slept.
The force of the blast hurled one of the window shutters onto
my bed, but it did not hit me.

These were the last days of our lives together as a family. One
year later, we were imprisoned in a detention camp in France.
Barbed wire fences, mud, hunger, and death. The family and the
world we knew were gone, never to return.

Before the Storm:
The Emergence of Nazism

Fred: Autumn 1933. We children (I was four years and old and Heinz-Menachem was one) were leading a very isolated life in the small village. We lived in the house opposite the synagogue, and Aunt Elsa, Father's sister, lived in the service apartment adjoining the synagogue. I don't remember much about that time, except for a small mouse under the bed, and a headless rooster that flew up into the air after it was killed.

Menachem: As we said, Aunt Elsa never married, but she had a son out of wedlock whose father was not Jewish. Our cousin Helmut was born in 1920. He was like a big brother to us. On November 13, 1939 he was sent to Paderborn concentration camp and forced to do backbreaking labor. Fate was not kind to him, and in May 1943, at the age of twenty-three, he was deported to Auschwitz and put to death.

Fred: Father was the part-time cantor to the shrinking community. I remember him leading the congregation in prayer during Friday evening and Sabbath day services. I also remember the Eternal Light gently swinging to and fro as it flickered above the Holy Ark containing the Torah scrolls. There were only a handful of worshippers. My brother and I sat on a bench in the front of the synagogue. The bench was really the cover of a chest containing Wimpels – strips of cloth, about twelve inches wide and six feet in length, used to bind up the Torah scrolls. It was an ancient German custom that when a child reached the age of three, the family would donate such a binder to the synagogue, elaborately decorated and embroidered with the child's name and family genealogy. The chest was full of them, reaching back to previous generations. While the grown-ups prayed, we children in our boredom rummaged through the chest and played with its hidden treasures, which included our own binders. They were all destroyed on Kristallnacht.

Menachem: I remember the bags of candies we kids received on one occasion – perhaps Simchat Torah?

Fred: I was six when I started school in 1935. In the spring of that year, I was enrolled in the local village elementary school, together with all the six-year-old non-Jewish children. One or two years later, I was forbidden to attend the local school when the Nazi government turned up the ratchet with its numerous prohibitions via the Nuremberg laws, making life as miserable as possible for the Jews, including their young children. I clearly remember my first day at school, wearing the square leather satchel, like a backpack, I had inherited from cousin Helmut. It held a board made of thin, flat slate, on which I wrote with chalk. We wrote on slate because it was cheaper than paper.

Walking to school was never pleasant. It was always a harrowing experience. German children were constantly indoctrinated and exposed to Nazi propaganda. They were brainwashed – their heads were filled with anti-Semitic ideas and racist attitudes. That's how the Hitler Youth came into being. Adults encouraged their youngsters to shun Jewish children. The bullies took this as approval to beat us up at every opportunity. And why not? After all, that's what the adults were doing.

Since I was the only Jewish kid in first grade, I was constantly subjected to harassment and beatings. Civics lessons were compulsory, but as a Jewish boy I was singled out by the teacher and asked to leave the classroom, a fact that was not lost on my schoolmates. I learned to run, to hide, and to duck the stones that flew at me. Most streets in the village were unpaved so there were plenty of pebbles and rocks lying about, and my knees were always bloodied and scabbed from frequent falls on sharp stones.

By the time I started school, all teachers not sympathetic to the Nazis had been purged. Menachem found out in recent years that my teacher was a senior Nazi in the local organization and was jailed after the war.

I do not recall a single incident where an adult, witnessing this daily bullying, tried to prevent the other kids from beating me up.

Menachem: One night in 1935, Eugen Laule, the council secretary, and Emile Hopp, the local Nazi party leader and village teacher, broke into the synagogue. Father heard the noise and went out to investigate. A fight broke out and Father was hurt. From sheer fright Aunt Elsa, who lived with us, fled to the backyard, where she found refuge in the cellar. Father told us he broke his nose falling off a wagon. I remember the backyard where Aunt Elsa hid – it was a garden of enchantment, with fruit trees and vegetables. I particularly recall the climbing beanstalks.

It was around that time that I was bitten by a dog. It happened like this: I was climbing the flight of stairs leading to the post office when I saw the tail of a dog wagging playfully in front of me. I grabbed hold and pulled hard. The startled dog spun around and clamped his teeth in my face. (Fred is certain it was he who pulled the dog's tail.) I was carried to the doctor in nearby Sinsheim, and I still remember how I screamed when I saw his scissors, which frightened me far more than the pain of the bite. The doctor didn't try to calm me down by explaining that he needed them to cut the bandage, not my face. Why bother explaining to children? They're only kids, not real people. Later I drew my own conclusions from that incident: children must be related to as complete human beings! In order to understand another person one must put oneself in his shoes, relating to each topic from his point of view. I have tried to apply these principles throughout my life. They have helped me immeasurably in my professional work as an educator and compiler of textbooks.

Fred: Hoffenheim was a small farming village and so it remains to this day. Unlike farm life in the United States, the farmers' homes were clustered in the village. Each day they would go to the outlying fields surrounding the village to work. Some of the farmhouses had stalls for cows on the ground floor with the family's living quarters on the upper floor. In the early years, we would visit with the neighbors before it became too risky for them to associate with us. I can still recall the gentle animal warmth and not unpleasant smells drifting to the upper floors from the cows below. The small Elsenz river flowed through the village. On hot days we kids paddled in the cool water, but when "our enemies" spotted us it was an open invitation, everyone yelling "drown the Jew boys." They would jump on me and hold my head under water, but at the very last moment they would let me go. Since that time I have been afraid of deep water… I can swim but I like the assurance that I can walk out.

Menachem: Once they caught me, too, in the same place. It happened in 1938. They beat me up and shoved me into a clump of nettles growing on the riverbank.

Fred: A communal garden was set aside along both sides of the narrow river. It was divided into plots, for the use of the poorest people of the village. We had one of those plots. In my mind's eye, I see Mother tilling the earth and watering the vegetables. That picture is one of my few happy memories of my birthplace. Mother was about thirty-eight then, with long brown hair down to her waist. I see her standing in the garden in the late afternoon hours… When I say "my birthplace," the German word Heimat resonates within me, with its powerful connotations of "belonging." In all the years since, I have never found an answer to the question: "Where is your home?" – it certainly isn't Hoffenheim!

On January 1, 1939, the screws were tightened further. Jews were forbidden to work in their professions, Jewish shops were closed or forced to be sold at bargain prices to non-Jews. Father, who was a cattle trader (a very common Jewish trade in that region), was suddenly unemployed. He and the other Jewish men were forced to do physical labor for the town, breaking rocks for the roads in the vicinity. For this work they were paid subsistence wages of a few marks.

Everyone was desperate to leave – but there was nowhere to go, especially for those with no money or connections. Despite this sorry state of affairs, our parents applied for visas to the United States, to join a relative, Adolph Heumann, who after the war would sponsor me to come to the United States. The emigration policy at that time was stringent in the extreme. Each country had a strict quota. Our application number was approximately 1,600,000 – apparently the subject was discussed at great length both at home and in the community, which is why I still remember the number. By the time of our deportation, number 900,000 had been called to the U.S. consulate. I guess the most common questions of the time were "How many will be approved?" "Which number has been called?" and "When will it be our turn?"

Menachem: I don't remember anything at all about this.

Fred: I remember several incidents from those days. I loved the barber's shop, because when I sat in his chair I could see storks nesting on the roof of the building across the way. They flew back and forth, feeding their chicks with frogs and other small creatures. One day, when Mother was away, I decided my brother needed a haircut. I don't know what possessed me, but I took Heinz to the barber, telling him to cut off the long blond hair that fell in ringlets to his shoulders and give him a real boy's haircut. That evening the two of us went to the station to meet Mother. As she emerged from the station she looked around for Heinz and asked me where he was. I replied: "Here he is, right next to me." I don't recall the consequences of that particular prank, but spankings were not unheard of in those days!

Menachem: You were probably jealous. As you said, I had gorgeous hair. Interestingly, I always thought that haircut was my idea, and I seem to remember waiting for Mother on the steps outside our house.

Fred: Another incident involved unripe apples. The road between our village and Sinsheim, the county seat, was lined with fruit trees – apples, pears, and plums. We enjoyed stealing and eating the fruit before it ripened. We picked them, took one bite and threw them away. Whenever a vehicle passed we tried to hit it and sometimes even succeeded. I can still see the apple splattering against the front door of a car painted with a swastika. The car continued on past us, stopped, reversed and came to a halt.

The door opened and two Nazi officers emerged in black uniforms and shiny boots. They wanted to know whether we threw an apple at them. We stoutly denied any such thing. They took down our particulars, threatened us ("you haven't heard the last of this") and continued on their way. Luckily for us, it never occurred to them that the two blond, blue-eyed urchins could be Jewish – we looked like purebred Aryans. They were true to their word, and that very same evening, when we came home, Father asked "what have you done?" It was useless to deny it. To this day I remember the beating that followed. My brother Heinz, who was only six, saved himself by claiming that he was only watching me... I was older, after all, and it was my job to look after him and set a good example.

Menachem: I remember snowy winter days. The whiteness covering everything, frost blossoms on the windows, and the quiet... I was five or six, and I can see myself dragging the sled to the top of the hill, lying down headfirst, and flying down to the bottom, steering with my foot. I didn't know the meaning of the word "fear."

I can still hear Christmas carols ringing in my ears. I don't know if you can understand this, but even today I am often enchanted by those beautiful sounds. They evoke longings for a world that is no more.

The Nine-Year-Old Frequent Traveler

Fred: In May 1937, the Ministry of Education forbade Jewish children to attend public schools. This was one of the many restrictions imposed on the Jewish community, and which were progressively strangling it. The new law directly affected this particular seven-year-old. After spending one year, first grade, in the village elementary school, I then had to attend a Jewish school in Heidelberg, some 20 kilometers away. I had to cover the distance by train every day, leaving early in the morning. The train stopped at each station on its way to the big city, so the entire journey lasted about one hour. This was quite an adventure; a bit scary at first, but I got used to it.

Seen through the eyes of a simple country lad the big city was full of wonders and surprises. They even had electric trams in the streets! I thoroughly enjoyed that daily trip and soon I made friends with the locomotive engineer and the conductor. I was probably the youngest regular traveler on the train. Inside my school bag was a thermos of hot soup prepared by Mother for my lunch (to this day I am very partial to soup). I did not receive pocket money.

Best of all, on the train I was anonymous – nobody knew who I was. From the time I got on nobody knew I was Jewish! Nobody beat me up, no one bothered me! In those days people didn't greet one another by saying "Good morning" but raised their right arm with the words "Heil Hitler." I unhesitatingly did the same. For that moment I, too, belonged!

School was boring. I don't remember what I learned or whether we ever had to do homework. Every now and again one of the local kids took me home for lunch. Towards evening I returned to the station, made my "Heil Hitler" salute, and traveled home. This routine continued for over a year till the day of the infamous Kristallnacht.

Menachem: After Kristallnacht, I also participated in the daily journey to Heidelberg. I stopped attending first grade in the Hoffenheim school after only a few months, but I'd already had a taste of the beatings and torments dished out by the village boys. I don't remember the daily train rides. I do remember causing trouble for Manfred by opening the carriage door several times during the trip. I attended the school for nearly two years. I can't recall anything I was taught but evidently I learned to write and read in German. I remember the sound of the water being flushed down the school toilets – a technological marvel that had not yet reached our village – and school trips through the forest to the ancient castle on the hilltop.

The Nightmare Begins:
Kristallnacht

To understand the background to Kristallnacht we need to digress into a little more history. The Nuremberg Laws of 1935 prohibiting intermarriage between Jews and Germans, and the revocation of citizenship were part of a continuum of pressure by means of terror, to get Jews to leave. Many did, but others couldn't face a new land, or had no connections overseas, or had no money. Many thought the situation couldn't last and decided to tough it out. Whatever the reason, the Germans turned up the screws.

By mid-1938, the German plans for war were well advanced. They had swallowed up Austria by annexation, with enthusiastic Viennese support. Now Hitler started making threats against Czechoslovakia. That country had been created barely eighteen years earlier following the First World War. Various ethnic peoples were brought together out of the Austrian-Hungarian Empire. Ethnic Germans lived in the province of Sudetenland. The Germans claimed they were being mistreated by the government and wanted to take control of the area, by force if necessary. The Czechs refused and moved their army to the border.

More or less at the same time the heat was turned up on the Jews. Businesses had to be "Aryanized" – sold to Germans no later than December 1938 for pennies on the dollar. Jewish physicians were prohibited from treating Germans. Lawyers were disbarred. The Jews were put under the complete control of the police.

In September, British Prime Minister Neville Chamberlain met Hitler in Munich and caved in to his demand to take over a piece of Czechoslovakia – the Sudetenland. Despite the vociferous objections of the Czechs, the British gave in, trusting to Hitler's promise that it was all he wanted. To this day, "a Munich" stands for betrayal and abandonment. Less than six months later, Hitler would take over all of Czechoslovakia, and the die was cast for the Second World War. Nevertheless, Hitler's plan for war in September 1938 had misfired, and with it the drastic actions he had planned against the Jews.

But then an unexpected opportunity presented itself. On November 7, 1938, a Polish-Jewish student, 17-year-old Herschel Grynszpan, assassinated the Third Secretary in the German embassy in Paris, Ernst vom Rath. Grynszpan's parents, who had lived in Germany since 1914, had just been expelled back into the no-man's-land between Germany and Poland, along with another 50,000 Polish Jews. The Poles refused to let them in, while the Germans prevented them from returning. There was no food or shelter, conditions were appalling, and the people were in a terrible state. When Grynszpan heard what had happened to his parents, he went to the embassy to plead their case. When he was rebuffed, he took out a handgun and shot vom Rath. If only more had taken this kind of action in response to the atrocities... In Europe, and particularly in Germany, private possession of a firearm was strictly prohibited and punishable by death. Only governments could kill with impunity! The Nazis had a fit – a Jew taking action against the Master Race was unheard of!!! They decided to teach all the Jews a lesson.

Fred: The situation deteriorated as steadily and monotonously as water dripping on a rock. I can't comprehend why the adults did not lose their sanity. In July, a decree required all Jews to apply for an identification card to be carried at all times. We were under constant police surveillance. In August 1938, a new ordinance forced Jews to add the name Israel for males and Sarah for females as their middle names, to facilitate identification... At the beginning of the nineteenth century, Jews were forbidden to give their children "Christian" names, by order of the Prussian authorities – who says history doesn't repeat itself?

I remember all of us – Mother, Heinz, and myself – going to the office in Sinsheim about four kilometers away, that dealt with these matters, to obtain our new identity cards. A large "J" was stamped on the gray certificate identifying us as Jews. I have no idea what happened to the certificate, whether it was lost or I destroyed it; but to this day I still have the photograph, embossed with a swastika.

Incidentally, the idea of superimposing a large "J" on the ID card was done at the request of the Swiss authorities. Yes, the admirable Swiss, those lovers of peace, order, and cleanliness, wrapped in the flag of the Red Cross – it was they who asked the Germans to adopt this means of identification so they could more easily recognize Jews trying to cross the border and send them back into the arms of the Gestapo. A few non-Jews also fled to Switzerland but they were willingly absorbed, and why not? After all, they were not Jewish.

Menachem: Sixty years later, in March 1999, while searching in the Karlsruhe archives, I came across a file containing the documents required to issue the new ID cards: questionnaires, photographs of our parents, and our own fingerprints. Don't the Germans ever throw anything away?

Fred: On the morning of November 9, 1938, I went to school as usual, but when I arrived, the teachers instructed me to go home at once. As I hurried home from the train station, I saw Mother pushing a cart piled high with clothes and bedding. In reply to my question she explained that they were destroying the synagogue and the adjacent apartment. Furniture and household objects lay scattered in the street. Father and the other men had been arrested and sent to Dachau concentration camp. Mother was on her way to the home of a relative, where we stayed until we were deported, two years later. I don't remember what I said to Mother. I ran to the place where our house had been – the synagogue. A crowd of people was milling around. Some local Nazis – including those who had been in school with my father, his comrades-in-arms during the First World War – were standing up above, on the roof, which they were busy dismantling with great enthusiasm. The pleasure with which they applied themselves to their work was painful to see. A few hours later, only a pile of rubble remained of the synagogue, which was built in 1750.

Menachem: I stood in the street, watching the rioters hurl our furniture out of the second floor window. Ten years later, in 1948, the local leader of the Nazis who ordered the destruction of the synagogue was brought to trial. I found the trial records in Yad Vashem: On Thursday, November 10, 1938, at 7:00 a.m., a directive was issued by the mayor of Sinsheim, and Emile Hopp, teacher and regional SA commander in Hoffenheim (the same man who taught Manfred in the local elementary school and who broke into the synagogue in 1935), instructed five or six local SA men to report in uniform to the synagogue, where Father met them. The Nazis ordered him to vacate our apartment because they were about to demolish the synagogue. They couldn't burn it for fear that fire would spread to nearby homes. The Germans tossed items of furniture from the second-floor windows. One of the SA men tried to help carry our personal belongings out of the building but he was prevented from so doing by his commanding officer who declared: "I will personally kick your butt if you help the Jews! This is your chance to prove you are a loyal Nazi." The uniformed men, assisted by local villagers, then entered the synagogue and methodically began to destroy it. The great chandelier came crashing to the ground, Torah scrolls and holy books were ripped, and the roof of the building was smashed. After everything had been wrecked, the shattered remains were loaded onto a wagon and carted off to an open field in the direction of Sinsheim, where they were burned. In a German court on June 11, 1948, sentences were handed down for Eugene Laule and Emile Hopp, the two ringleaders – Laule was jailed for fourteen months and Hopp for eleven weeks.

Fred: At the end of a full day of riots, Father was taken from us and imprisoned in Dachau concentration camp for a month.

When the prisoners arrived at the camp their heads were shaved and they were dressed in prison garb. Some three hundred men were crammed into huts intended for forty men. They spent hours standing in the freezing rain. Tormented and degraded, they were subjected to the capricious whims of the SS. Not long ago, at Yad Vashem, we uncovered a record of Father's incarceration in Dachau. He was released earlier than others because of "concessions" made to German veterans of World War I!

Menachem: On November 9, 1938, German streets were ablaze. That night and the following day became known as Kristallnacht – a reference to the shards from shattered chandeliers, windows, and glass that lay strewn everywhere. More than 1,300 synagogues and public institutions and 7,000 Jewish businesses were destroyed in one day. At least one hundred Jews were killed. Thousands more were injured, degraded and humiliated, and some 30,000 men were arrested and imprisoned in concentration camps.

Fred: When Menachem and I returned to Hoffenheim in 1990, the locals proudly showed us the memorial plaque that had been set up in honor of the vanished Jewish community.

Menachem: The plaque was mounted on a wall in the local Christian cemetery, in a corner dedicated to those who fell during the World Wars. Beneath a carved relief of a menorah and several crosses was inscribed: In memory of the victims of the Nationalist-Socialist regime, 1933-1945. I was doubly horrified – both by the location of the plaque and by the inscription.

I asked the young pastor who accompanied us, a man of forty or thereabouts, why the brass plaque had been set up here rather than in the center of the community, at the site where Germans had demolished the synagogue. The priest replied that the authorities forbade it. I asked why there was no specific reference to the Jewish community? Why the entwined symbols? What was the significance of the crosses and why was there no Star of David? How could a German child identify a menorah?

Why the distortion of the truth? Embarrassed he replied: "That's all the authorities permitted." I retorted that coming generations cannot be taught distorted half-truths.

Life at 10 Kirchstrasse

Fred: After witnessing the destruction of the synagogue, I went to the home of Ida and Herman Heumann, relatives on Father's side (the maiden name of his mother, our grandmother, was Heumann. I think that Heumann's mother and our grandmother were sisters). The address was 10 Kirchstrasse (Church Street), the house next to the church. Before the war, the Heumanns owned the kosher butchery where, as I already mentioned, Father was apprenticed in his youth. Mother went ahead of us, hauling a cart piled high with our belongings, and we moved in with them the same day. We all slept in the same room – Mother, six-year-old Heinz and myself. I was nine. When Father returned from the concentration camp, there were four of us living in that room.

Father returned from Dachau on December 8. He and the others were released early because of their military service during the First World War. Father was in a dreadful state – missing one shoe, with his leg in bandages. He didn't tell us much about his experiences of the past four weeks. At the time, he was forty-four years old.

Menachem: Father told us about the abuse he suffered at the hands of the SS – standing to attention in the parade ground, the "frog leaps" they were forced to do for hours...

Fred: In earlier years, I remember having watched in secret the animals being slaughtered, although the adults made every effort to keep us away. Watching that mysterious killing was irresistible to us children. Today I avert my head when it happens in movies.

Menachem: By the time we moved in with the Heumanns, there was no kosher slaughtering. It was banned in 1933, and there is no doubt that the Jews obeyed the edict.

Fred: They also had a dog in a wire enclosure. He was a large, black and brown beast – a Rottweiler. He hated me. Every time I passed by he hurled himself against the bars, barking in a frenzy. I was terrified of him.

Menachem: Actually I got on fine with him. We used to play together...

I have several memories of Kirchstrasse 10: gazing in wonder at Zeppelins (airships) floating across the sky; the blue-and-white box of the Jewish National Fund on the sideboard in the living room – I can still recall the rattling sound it made. I remember the melody of a Zionist song "Dieses schone Land am blauen Meeres Strand."[4] Is that where my Zionist roots come from?

Fred: The house in Kirchstrasse is still standing today, in the shadow of the Protestant church in Hoffenheim. I still remember the ringing of its bells. For a Jewish child, the church was a place of mystery, frightening and intriguing at the same time. I badly wanted to look inside, but I knew very well what the Hitler Youth would do if they caught me there. Today, I still get pleasure from the sound of church bells, they send a shiver down my spine. Five years later, in France, I had to attend church every Sunday, pretending to be a devout Catholic, just to remain alive.

Life in the Heumann household was a tight fit with two families squeezed together, soon to be augmented by a third, when cousin Ingrid's family was forced to leave from the French border. Mr. Heumann suffered from frequent epileptic attacks; there was no way to control them. He would roll on the floor and thrash about as if struggling with an unseen demon. It was terrifying to watch.

---

4   The full translation appears on page 210.

The house was heated by a wood stove, but in winter the warmest place was the kitchen. Warm and comforting, it was there that all cooking and baking was done in a large wood-burning stove. Above the stove were hooks of various sizes for pots. The best place to sit was between the stove and the table. I remember once sitting at the table, waiting for the soup to heat on the stove. As Mrs. Heumann added more firewood through a hole in the stovetop, the pot toppled over, emptying the scalding soup on my thigh. I screamed like a pig being slaughtered. My winter clothes stuck to me and when they were removed the skin came away with them. Various portions of my right leg were badly burned; the pain was unbearable. I don't know what treatment they used for burns in those days, but it took three months for my leg to heal; to this day I have a large scar on my thigh. I will never forget the German doctor – the one who used to treat us before the prohibition. He risked his life, coming to us in secret at night to examine my injury. By that time it was forbidden for Aryan doctors to treat Jews.

Menachem: They made you lie in bed under the stairs leading to the bedrooms. I came to visit you there. I remember that you were burning up with fever and delirious...

The Gold Pocket Watch

Fred: One day in June 1939, a large wooden crate was brought into the living room. That's how we discovered that Aunt Elsa was immigrating to England! The packing began. Jews leaving Germany were not permitted to take jewelry, valuables, and of course, money, so a customs officer had to be present during packing. It was his job to prevent forbidden items from being included and to stamp each crate with a seal, indicating that everything was in order. We children stood around and watched the proceedings. Father knew the customs officer. The two of them chatted amiably, and every now and then a drink was offered and accepted. Within quite a short time, the officer was totally befuddled. My parents took the opportunity of slipping some silverware and a gold pocket watch into the crate. Thirty-one years later, when Aunt Elsa came to California on a visit in 1970, she brought me that gold watch. I wound the spring and it worked perfectly. Inside the watch cover were inscribed the dates when it had been repaired, beginning in the 1880s. The watch is the only family possession I have ever owned. In 1992, I gave it to my son David. Keep it safe, David.

The Winds of War

Hitler's early victories were greeted with flowers, not guns. The entries into the Rhineland, Austria, and the Sudetenland were adventures in diplomatic brinkmanship. Their success greatly encouraged further quests for *Lebensraum* (living space). In mid-March Hitler annexed Czechoslovakia. England and France made diplomatic noises, but nothing more.

A few days later, Neville Chamberlain, the British Prime Minister, realized that in Munich Hitler had deceived him when he declared that the annexation of the Sudetenland would be his final territorial demand. At the end of March, the British announced that if Poland was threatened they would come to her aid. The French added their assurances. This was prompted by demands that Hitler was starting to make for the return of the Polish city of Danzig. In April, he told the High Command of the German Army to prepare for the invasion of Poland, arguing that since he could not count on Polish neutrality in the case of war with England and France, Poland must be eliminated first… This must be a new definition of chutzpah!!!

The Russians under the dictatorship of Stalin watched all this with increasing unease. Poland was on their border. If war came, they were not prepared. Remember that after Jews, Hitler hated communists, and vice versa. Nevertheless, the Russians attempted to cut a deal with the Germans. For Hitler, this lifeline was heaven-sent. It would protect his rear in the event of a conflict with Britain and France. The two dictators who hated each other so much signed a pact of non-aggression, which only goes to prove that there is no honor among thieves. The world was aghast, astounded. It was unbelievable! But Hitler was deliriously happy. He was on top of the world, viewing himself as the greatest strategic genius since Napoleon – he had humbled the great British Empire and made Germany a country to be reckoned with once again, after its defeat in World War I.

In Charlie Chaplin's film, *The Great Dictator*, Chaplin plays Hitler. In one famous scene he jumps on his desk, takes a globe of the world, throws it into the air and dances with it. This must have been exactly how Hitler felt. He had the world by the – !

Emboldened, he ordered the German army to invade Poland on September 1, 1939. World War II had begun. Two days later, Britain and France declared war on Germany. Within four weeks, with lightening speed, the Germans defeated the Poles. By September 27 it was all over. The Russians and the Germans split Poland as per their agreements. In the process, some three million Polish Jews came under German control. On the Western front things were relatively calm. The British and French were fully mobilized but for six months nothing happened. Then in April 1940, the Germans overran Norway and Denmark, and in May, Holland, Belgium, and France. With the surrender of France on June 21, 1940, Hitler stood triumphant at the English Channel.

Fred: At the time, Hoffenheim, along with the rest of Germany, was ringing with the victories of the Wehrmacht (the regular army). The people were proud of their invincible army; consequently, they treated Jews more aggressively. Stones were thrown at us, hitting their mark on more than one occasion. I particularly remember one incident: I was walking in the street when a horse-drawn wagon passed. The driver, a farmer aged forty-five or so, lashed at me – a child of ten – with his whip, shouting "Go home to Palestine, cursed Jew!" If only we could have... I had welts all over.

Two other episodes from that time come to mind. Farmers were short of manpower because most of the able-bodied had been drafted into the army. I don't know whether we were compelled to work or whether we did it to make some money.

With our mother, we went to a farmer's field and picked peas. We put them into sacks tied over our shoulders. When the bags were full, we would take them to a wagon, have them weighed, and start over. This was not my idea of fun. The poor could glean the fields after the farmers had taken in their harvest – just like Ruth in the Bible. I distinctly remember gleaning potatoes and wheat stalks with our mother in the fields of the village. Things must have been harder than we children realized.

The day war broke out, all German Jews living near the French border were forced to leave for the interior. Uncle Moritz (Father's brother), his wife Alma, and their three-year-old daughter Ingrid came to live with us in Kirchstrasse. As far as I can remember we all lived together in that one room. No doubt the adults had many concerns and worries to occupy them in those days. They whispered together and we were often asked to leave the room – they had good reason to be deathly afraid. In January 1939 Hitler had announced: "We will destroy the Jews. This time we will not let them get away with what they did in November 1918." One week later, during the course of a speech at the Reichstag he declared:

> In the course of my life I have often been a prophet, and have usually been ridiculed for it. During the time of my struggle for power it was in the first instance the Jewish race which only received my prophecies with laughter when I said that I would one day take over the leadership of the State, and with it that of the whole nation, and that I would then among many other things settle the Jewish problem. Their laughter was uproarious, but I think that for some time now they have been laughing on the other side of their face. Today I will once more be a prophet: If the international Jewish financiers in and outside Europe should succeed in plunging the nations once more into a world war, then the result will not be the bolshevization of the earth, and thus the victory of Jewry, but the annihilation of the Jewish race in Europe![5]

---

5   Hitler's speech on January 30, 1939, quoted in: *Documents on the Holocaust*, Jerusalem, 1987, pp. 134–135.

These words were uttered eight months before the outbreak of the war. Maliciously, he was blaming a handful of Jews for starting the war, a war for which he had been agitating for many years, because clearly he had ulterior motives. Hitler had been hatching a diabolical plan to get rid of the Jews since the 1920s and he needed a war for cover. But at this time no human could possibly conceive or begin to imagine the dimensions and scope of the plan. It was, quite simply, "The Solution to the Jewish Problem." No matter how outrageous his words and deeds, many, many people believed him and joyously implemented his decisions. In fact, there was competition among the Nazi leadership as to who could make the Jews' life more miserable... it would get them a promotion.

Once the war started, we were trapped in Germany. It was still possible to leave, but only to neutral countries, and only on condition that one had the necessary permits, connections and, needless to say, money. We had none of these things.

Deportation to France

Fred: On October 22, 1940, a new and terrifying element entered our lives. At eight in the morning, two members of the Gestapo (secret police) presented themselves at the Heumanns' door and instructed us to be prepared to leave within two hours. We were permitted to take up to fifty kilograms of personal effects per adult and thirty per child, and one hundred marks each. That's all the information we received – they didn't reveal our destination and they certainly didn't explain why it had become necessary for us to leave our home. We were stunned. The announcement was totally unexpected, like a bolt from the blue. At the time, there were six adults living in the house: Herman and Ida Heumann, aged fifty-eight; Father, forty-six, and Mother, forty-two; Uncle Moritz, forty-four, and his wife Alma, thirty; and there were three children: I was eleven, Heinz eight, and Ingrid three years old. All the Jews of Hoffenheim were deported that same day.

How clearly I remember Mother frenziedly packing everything she could lay her hands on in a large bamboo trunk. The Gestapo men watched in silence with expressionless faces. I can still see the hand of one man resting on the barrel of his pistol. I thought he would shoot... Father spoke excitedly with one of them – I don't recall what he said, but I distinctly remember him taking out his distinguished service awards, including the Iron Cross, and angrily throwing them at the feet of the Gestapo. They were embarrassed and remained silent.

Menachem: I remember Father shouting: "Is this why I fought in the war?"

Fred: The Gestapo walked us through the village of our birth to the town hall, where open trucks awaited us. The community, seventeen of us, young and old, were loaded onto the trucks and taken to the railway station at Heidelberg.

Menachem: In December 1988, I unexpectedly received the following letter:

> Dear Heinz,
> This is Paul, the boy from the neighbors' backyard. Do you remember me? I left Hoffenheim 37 years ago. When I was talking to my family recently they told me you had visited Hoffenheim. I wept, because I always thought none of you remained alive. I used to get used clothes and toys from you and Manfred.[6] We were a very poor family of seven and we were always grateful for the things you gave us. I remember your parents and Manfred very well. Manfred was a strong kid, not like you and me. We used to play together. I remember you coming out of your house carrying matzos, and you shared them with me.
>
> I remember very well the day you were deported. You stood next to your mother, behind the wagon. It was very cold that morning and I wanted to bring you a blanket, but they didn't let me... The village mayor didn't permit it. He said to my mother: "Louisa, I don't want to see your boy playing with Jews." I'm writing to tell you that I've always thought about you.

When we visited Hoffenheim in 1992, we met a young theology student named Ludwig Streib. In the course of his studies he wrote a paper on "The Hoffenheim Jewish Community 1918–1945." One hundred pages in length, it contains some fascinating details

6   He was referring to the period before we were deported.

about the community, our family, and us personally. Streib was hoping we would be able to contribute some personal data for his thesis, but in fact we gained even more from him – a vast hoard of information about events and details of which we were unaware. Among other things, he tracked down Manfred's school registration and a photograph of myself in the local nursery school. His paper deals with Hitler's rise to power and describes the attitudes, conduct, and reactions of the local population, the church, and the authorities towards the Jews. The work focuses primarily on the early stages – Kristallnacht, deportation, and what followed. He based his research on interviews with the local population who were still alive in 1988 and 1989 and who were prepared to talk about their feelings at that time. It's incredible to me how selective one's memory can be!!!

This is how Streib describes the deportation:

> At noon the 17 members of the small Jewish community assembled at the town hall. Most knew what would happen to them… [*he was wrong; we had no idea. M.M.*]. A woman met Mr. and Mrs. Heumann as they were carrying their suitcases to the town hall. She describes the scene as follows: "I said to them, 'Goodbye Mrs. Heumann, Goodbye Herman.' With him I used the familiar form 'Du' because I knew him as a small child. He responded, 'They should all drop dead, all in one pile…' Mrs. Heumann said, 'Herman, be quiet. You can't change anything.' He responded, 'I don't give a damn, we're not going somewhere where things are better!'"

Very few neighbors accompanied the Jews to the town hall. The trucks arrived and uniformed men shoved and pushed the Jews aboard. A Hoffenheimer who was standing around said to a Nazi, "Why don't you go to war? There you could do some good! These people haven't done you any harm!" The fellow in uniform replied, "You are right, but if you don't keep your mouth shut, you will end up in Dachau (concentration camp) as well." Nothing further is known of the local population's reaction.

Streib continues:

The Jews of Hoffenheim, together with the Jews of neighboring villages, were trucked to Heidelberg, where they were put into special trains. The trains left the same day, passing various towns in Baden on their way to the French border town of Mulhouse, where the one hundred marks were changed for French currency. The SS warned that anyone holding more than one hundred marks would be shot, and the same fate awaited anyone who attempted to leave the train. Nine special trains departed the Gau (district) of Baden for southern France. After several days without food or water, their future shrouded in a fog of uncertainty, the trains stopped at the foothills of the Pyrenees, near Gurs close to the French-Spanish border.

Streib's description matches our recollections.[7]

On the evening of the day we were deported, October 22, Robert Wagner, governor of the Baden district, proudly notified Berlin that "the district of Baden is the first German district to be *Judenrein*" – cleansed of Jews. This concept was very dear to the hearts of the Nazis – not "free of Jews" but "cleansed of Jews."

Fred: Wagner, the regional commandant, was a fanatical Nazi. His determination to deport the Jews as fast as possible was what, in fact, saved the two of us, because we were sent west rather than east. Two years later, all the other members of our family were transported to Auschwitz and killed. Only we survived – by a miracle.

Menachem: On October 29, the SS commander, Heydrich, issued the following communication. It can also be seen as a reflection

---

7   Streib, Ludwig, *Die Israelitische Gemeinde iti Hoffenheim, 1919–1945*, unpublished MS, 1989.

of the lack of concern displayed by local people – both German and French – towards Nazi actions:

Berlin, 29 October 1940
To: The Appointed Authority

For the attention of SA Commander Luther, Berlin

The Fuhrer has ordered the deportation of all Jews of Baden by way of Alsace and the Jews of the Palatinate by way of Lorraine. At the conclusion of this mission I am pleased to report that on October 22 and 23 seven transports departed from Baden and two from the Palatinate.

6,505 Jews

The matter was coordinated with local military bodies but without prior knowledge of the French authorities. The trains passed through unoccupied territory to Chalon-sur-Saone. The deportation of Jews from Baden and the Palatinate was conducted smoothly and no problems were encountered. The operation attracted no particular attention among the populace. The relevant official bodies are handling confiscated Jewish property. Jews of mixed marriages were not included in these transports.

Heydrich[8]

The Journey to Gurs

Fred: The train carriages were intended for passengers. They were not cattle cars. I remember an SS man entering our carriage and demanding all the valuables in our possession. The train traveled slowly and stopped frequently. Of the journey itself I remember little.

---

8   Archiv Auswertiges Amt, Bonn, file K204459.

Menachem: The train stopped somewhere. An announcement was made over the loudspeaker, in German of course: "Anyone descending from the train or putting his head out of the window will be shot!" I was terrified by the shouts. Being young and small, I was put to sleep in a kind of hammock – a netting above the benches, intended for luggage.

On October 25, 1940, after traveling for a long time, the train arrived in pouring rain at the station of a small French town, Oloron-Ste.-Marie, not far from Pau, in the foothills of the Pyrenees. Uncovered trucks ferried the deportees to their new location. When it was our turn, we were taken to the Gurs detention camp, where we met Grandmother Mina and Uncle Emanuel.

Menachem: We were in a place surrounded by barbed wire, with lots of wooden barracks. These were originally intended for Spanish prisoners, refugees from the Civil War in neighboring Spain. (France had built at least a dozen of these types of camps to incarcerate political prisoners.) Other groups came later. Upon arrival, men and women were separated. The younger children were permitted to remain with their mothers, so we stayed with Mother.

For many of the deportees, this was the gateway to death. A quarter of the Jews from Baden incarcerated in Gurs died in the camps in France (1,168 out of 4,464 – 26.2 percent); nearly half (2,028 – 45.1 percent) were sent on to death camps – Auschwitz or Majdanek. Of those, only 13(!) survived. All told, 71.3 percent of the deportees of October 22, lost their lives. Of those who survived, 491 (11.0 percent) managed to escape from France, and 777 (17.4 percent) remained hidden in that country.

The French Response

Our deportation to France and imprisonment in the camp took place some four months after France signed the armistice with Germany. The terms stipulated that Germany would have military control of the northern, industrial section of the country and the Atlantic littoral, with France continuing to rule over the south. The Gurs camp, situated in southern France several kilometers from the Spanish border, was under full French control. Vichy was the capital city of the unoccupied zone.

The Vichy government was taken by surprise by the German decision to deport 6,500 Jews to the area, and consequently they were entirely unprepared. A formal protest was lodged through the armistice committee, but Vichy's protest was mainly intended to avoid later repercussions, and as such it did not make any impression on the German regime – the German Foreign Ministry simply filed away the document.

During the entire period of our stay in Gurs we never saw a single German. In other words, we were political prisoners held by the French under disgraceful conditions. Armed French guards patrolled the camp and kept watch on the gates and fences. Naturally, the camp commander was a French officer.

Why did the French agree to absorb this tattered remnant, none of whom spoke a word of French? Why didn't they let them escape? Why did they collaborate with the Germans? And why did they do the Nazis' dirty work for them? After all, the Vichy government could have unlocked the gates and allowed us all to disappear. At the time, the Germans really didn't care what became of us.

French postwar governments have never fully accounted for Vichy's role in the Holocaust, neither to themselves nor to the world. The French saw themselves as victims of the Nazis, not perpetrators. However, in recent years a change has come about. The current governments have finally admitted the complicity of the Vichy regime. Many of the public collaborated, but large numbers also resisted; that's why we survived.

For years we wondered why the Nazis deported this group of Jews to the west, to France, and not east to Poland where the Final Solution was implemented. Based on research, we have concluded that in 1940, when we were deported, the intention was to get rid of the Jews – anywhere. The idea of wholesale mass murder was still dormant; it had not completely matured. Instead the Nazis resorted to a somewhat older idea to resettle the Jews on a reservation somewhere in Africa. One of the reservations being explored was the then-French colony of Madagascar.

In a memorandum by Himmler, head of the SS, to Hitler in May 1940, he writes: "I hope to see the concept of Jews completely obliterated, with a large migration of all Jews to Africa or else in a colony."

A Way Station to Madagascar?

Now that France was conquered, Heydrich, head of the SS Police, and Eichmann, head of Jewish Affairs, considered the time propitious to implement the program. The German Armistice Commission and the Delegation of the Unoccupied Territory representing the Vichy regime had already held discussions to deport the French Jews of Alsace and Lorraine to the southern part of France. Alsace and Lorraine were French provinces adjoining Germany. They had been handed back and forth many times, depending on who won which war. People in these provinces spoke French and German. The Nazis had appointed Robert Wagner as *Gauleiter* (Governor) over our native province of Baden. He was also put in charge of Alsace. Similarly, Josef Bürkel, *Gauleiter* for the Palatinate, took charge of Lorraine. They interpreted their directive from Heydrich literally and not only deported the French Alsace/Lorraine Jews into southern France, but also those from their German provinces.

We mentioned earlier that in spite of the German reputation for efficiency, they did screw up once in a while. It's quite conceivable and has in fact been suggested that we were not meant to be deported at that time... who knows?

Wagner and Bürkel were more Nazi than most, the type of which Goldhagen wrote so eloquently in *Hitler's Willing Executioners*. Yet Wagner's ambitiousness most likely saved our lives, since we were deported west before being redeported east to Auschwitz,

like all the members of our family some eighteen months later...
Such is fate.

What was the Vichy reaction to having nearly 7,000 Jews
dumped on them? Streib, in his paper, writes:

> The Vichy regime was totally surprised and unprepared. They
> protested and ordered that the transport be returned (we presume
> at the border), but this made little impression on the German
> administration.[9]

A different source says: "Vichy protested through the Armistice
Commission. The German Ministry of Foreign Affairs pigeonholed
the protest so as not to create complications for the deportation
authorities. But the deportation which Heydrich and Eichmann
hoped to extend to the 270,000 Jews still in the Reich was not
continued. It was unwise to offend the Vichy government too
much."[10]

They accepted and received its voluntary cooperation later.

This signaled the end of the Madagascar Plan. It was an
aberration in the path to the Final Solution, which was shortly
to be implemented.

For the moment, we were in the concentration camp of Gurs.
What was it like to live behind barbed wire?

Life in Gurs Detention Camp

Fred: The year is 1940. Winter. Rain, wind, damp and cold...
The barracks they put us in were completely bare. That first
night we didn't even have straw to sleep on. It was a far cry from
home, from our more-or-less normal lives, to this entirely new
reality; the contrast was so stark that we were all in shock. After

---

9   Streib, *Die Israelitische Gemeinde in Hoffenheim*.
10   Leon Poliakov, *Harvest of Hate – the Nazi Program for the
     Destruction of the Jews of Europe*, Philadelphia 1954.

a few days, the adults began to comprehend the magnitude of the calamity that had befallen them. The little ones and the old people simply cried and whimpered all the time.

Menachem: There were altogether three hundred large wooden barracks, built to house 20,000 people. The camp was divided into thirteen "islands" – *îlots* – to the French, designated by the letters of the alphabet – each comprising between twenty-five and twenty-eight units. Each island was surrounded by barbed wire and guarded by French sentries. Our island, Ilot I, certainly was an island – we were separated and isolated from the others … as well as from the outside world beyond the camp fence.

The barrack was about thirty meters long and seven meters wide. There was a door at either end. The windows were wooden shutters that could be opened, giving rise to many arguments. It was too hot for one, too cold for another, the third person complained about too much light…

Fred: When the two of us – eleven and eight years old – went outside in the morning, we immediately sank into mud, because the entire camp was built on swampland. There were no sidewalks, no pavement or vegetation – just a sea of squelching mud. I do not exaggerate when I say that it came up to my knees, and it was hard work dragging out anyone who had the misfortune to fall in. The mud was a severe hindrance, especially for the old people, who found it almost impossible to get to the toilet facilities. Everyone who survived clearly remembers the mud of Gurs.

Life in the camp centered around eating and finding shelter. For washing there was cold water, running from crude pipes drilled with small holes, and located out in the open. That winter was exceptionally severe, and the water often froze in the pipes. The temperature in Gurs, in the foothills of the Pyrenees, plummeted to below minus four Fahrenheit. Washing under these conditions may have suited boy scouts, but it was a calamity for the old people, as well as the women who were forced to wash themselves in public without a shred of privacy. We children were not bothered too much – we weren't too fond of washing anyway.

The toilets were another story. They were installed next to the barbed wire fence surrounding the camp. To get to them you had to climb some stairs to a flat slab of concrete cemented to pillars. Along the entire length of this slab were holes, separated from one another by low partitions and open to the heavens. The only way to relieve oneself was to squat over these holes and take aim! If you hit the target, well and good, if not... Naturally, the whole area became contaminated and befouled within a very short time. The stench was unbearable. Under each hole was a barrel, holding between fifty and one hundred liters. Every morning it was the task of the Spanish prisoners to remove the full barrels and replace them with empty ones. This was done by means of carts on a narrow rail track running around the perimeter of the camp, which we children promptly named the "shithouse express."

When we arrived in the camp in October 1940, we were supervised by German non-Jewish female prisoners. They had fled from Germany to France because of their anti-Nazi views. At the start of the war between France and Germany, they were imprisoned as enemy aliens by the French and found themselves in Gurs. They spoke both French and German, so some of them were appointed to take charge of the barracks that had been suddenly inundated with this German-speaking humanity. One of them was Hanna Schramm. After the war she wrote a book, *Living in Gurs*, wherein she described the day we arrived:

> The first ones to emerge from the darkness into the lighted hut were old women, women holding babies, others leading children by the hand, all of them wide-eyed with fear. The trucks arrived one after the other, unloading their cargo – women of all ages, rich women, poor women, the healthy and the sick. There were many children with them and elderly people of 95... They looked like ghosts, confused and bewildered, in an unfamiliar world... It was

raining the night they landed in Gurs, in the mud and the pollution, to be thrust into miserable huts, worse than prison cells.[11]

The Jewish organizations and various welfare associations, Jewish and non-Jewish alike, were informed of the dreadful conditions in the camp; in 1941, they began distributing food supplements. Adam Rotkowsky wrote: "There is severe hunger...we must save these people...we must act now... Organizations such as the Oeuvre de Secours aux Enfants (OSE), the Quakers, ORT, the Joint Distribution Committee, YMCA, the American Red Cross, Secours Suisse, CAR, and Hicem have all tried to help."

But it was too little and too late for the elderly and the feeble. The Gurs cemetery is the final resting place for 1,187 camp prisoners, including Grandmother Mina. She was seventy-two when she died (1870-1942). Some time after the war, tombstones were erected. Grandmother Mina's grave is number 562, as I learned thirty years later during one of my pilgrimages.

Lice were everywhere. There were frequent outbreaks of diphtheria, typhoid fever, dysentery, and other infectious diseases. The children received various inoculations. For some reason I still have my inoculation certificate listing all those painful shots.

The food was minimal, totally inadequate to say the least – ersatz coffee, slices of black bread... We can't remember receiving real solid food. We were given watery soup in which a few cabbage leaves floated. The lucky ones found a lump of potato or carrot in their ladle of soup, and the greatest joy imaginable was the discovery of some shreds of meat. We were always hungry. The food was cooked in huge pots over an open flame, in the kind of field kitchen that was in common use among armies in the nineteenth century.

Menachem: Always hungry, we kids ran wild in the camp. It didn't take long for us to find our way to the other blocks (islands),

---

11 Schramm Hanna, *Vivre à Gurs*, Paris 1979.

where Father and our uncles were being held. Visits to Father were even more special, because he had been drafted as a cook for his barbed-wire enclosure. If you have to be a prisoner, this must be the best occupation in the whole camp. Father was always looking for work and, possibly because of his past experience as a butcher, he was assigned to the kitchen. The kitchen was a makeshift structure – several poles holding up a sheet of tin. Over an open fire stood a long row of barrels that functioned as enormous cooking-pots.

Fred: During our sneak visits Father would cut us a thick slice from a round loaf of bread, toast it over the open flame, and spread it with a thick layer of fat from a large 5-gallon tin can. He sprinkled brown sugar on top. What joy! There was simply no better gift he could make to his sons. This addition to our daily ration helped us survive. I remember this very clearly because those moments were so precious… food, and then more food… It is impossible for anyone who has not experienced true hunger to understand how important food became to us, and how central it was to our lives.

Menachem: There was no school. We spent the whole day roaming around the camp. I remember hiding behind a hut and smoking cigarette butts picked out of the mud!

Fred: We also explored the area outside the camp. We got as far as the nearby village of Gurs. The French police never stopped us – they knew we'd eventually return to our parents in the camp. I can't remember how we managed to communicate with them – we didn't speak a word of French! We were pretty wild kids, taking full advantage of our enforced "vacation" behind barbed wire.

One morning, I awoke to see two candles burning beside me. A woman had died in the night. It was the first time I saw a dead body. The Spanish prisoners who were responsible for cleaning the camp came by with a cart every morning to collect the Angel of Death's gleanings of the previous night.

Menachem: I remember standing next to the fence one morning, transfixed by the sight of a horse-drawn wagon carrying corpses covered with blankets, as it moved through the camp. I can still see the legs sticking out.

Separation

Menachem: We kids didn't know that various people and organizations were trying to get children out of the camp. One day, our parents told us they had given their permission for us to be taken from the camp – together with other children – to a children's home somewhere in France. They explained that it would be better for us, because camp conditions were intolerable. We would be given more food… We don't remember how we felt or how we reacted to this news. On the morning of February 24, four months after arriving in the camp, we climbed into a truck that took us to the Oloron train station.

Fred: I remember Father standing next to the truck – he sobbed as he made me promise to look after my younger brother, not yet nine years old.

Menachem: I remember Father lifting me into the truck and gazing into my eyes. I imagine he said something like "Be a good boy and listen to your big brother." I can't really remember his face, but I still see his eyes – large, blue, and very sad. We didn't have a chance to say goodbye to Mother because the truck didn't wait, but I can still see her standing on the wooden bridge and waving as the truck passed.

None of us could ever have imagined that we would never meet again.

We keep asking ourselves how they found the inner strength to send their sons, twelve and not yet nine, into the unknown. Their bravery seems all the greater when we consider that they were in the minority – most of the parents, unable to foresee what lay ahead, refused to part with their children. All of them perished in Auschwitz.

Fred: When I think of my children and grandchildren I can't help but wonder how our parents found the courage to do what they did.

Menachem: That's right: I only began to think about it when my grandchildren reached the same age. That's when I appreciated their heroism.

Fred: I only have one answer – living conditions in the camp were so appalling that to send us away may have seemed the lesser of two evils.

Menachem: Andrée Salomon, a social worker for the OSE, took us out of the camp. A few years ago, when we met in Jerusalem, she told me she persuaded our parents to let us go by assuring them we would have plenty of food on the outside. It was their concern for us that gave them the strength to do what they did.

We already mentioned that various organizations were active in the Gurs camp. Among them was OSE, a Jewish association for saving children,[12] whose chief purpose at this time was to protect and save Jewish children. Their rescue program was carried out with the assistance of other organizations, so our transfer from Gurs was undertaken with the help of the Quaker organization, the American Friends Service Committee.

Andrée Salomon was the OSE representative. She found places for forty-eight children: we were taken to an orphanage – Maison des Pupilles de la Nation – an institution in Aspet, in southern France, not far from the town of St.-Gaudens. The orphanage

---

12 Organisation de Secours aux Enfants – the children's welfare organization.

was one of several that had been established by the French government after the First World War (in which 1.4 million Frenchmen lost their lives) for children whose widowed mothers were no longer able to take care of them. Now, twenty years later, these orphanages were relatively empty.

Fred: Until recently my knowledge of the events leading up to our departure was incomplete, but during one of our conversations, Menachem told me about the letter he received from a Quaker activist, Ms. Alice Resch. Here is what she writes about the events prior to our leaving Gurs:

Ms. Helga Holbeck, head of the delegation of American Friends, heard about the arrival of the German deportees to Gurs. Madeline Barot, who headed CIMADE,[13] the Protestant welfare association, had, unbeknownst to the authorities, already spent some months in the camp. Helga Holbeck asked Madeline how the Quakers could help. They visited Gurs and decided to distribute food supplements.

Ms. Holbeck immediately grasped the children's plight. Upon her return to Toulouse she contacted Andrée, together with the Pau district governor, and the camp authorities... Helga worked with the governor in Toulouse.[14] ... It took some time for this administrative activity to bear fruit. Persuading the parents also took time. We were finally able to convince them that the children would be better off outside the camp, where they would receive food and perhaps attend school... We also hoped the parents would be able to visit their children...

Andrée Salomon and a couple named Cohen accompanied the children in the truck, first to Oloron, then by train to St.-Gaudens and again by truck to Aspet. There Andree took her leave of us, after giving the necessary documents to Mr. Couvot, director of the orphanage. Mr. Couvot, who knew not a word of German, was left

---

13 Comité intermouvements auprès des evacués.
14 To this day, France is divided into ninety-five departments (cantons), each with its own governor, appointed by the central government.

with forty-eight children who knew not a word of French. Panic-stricken, he immediately phoned the Quaker office in Toulouse: "Help! Send someone who speaks German." Helga asked me whether I would travel to Aspet, and off I went, with my stomach in a knot! It was one thing to distribute food and clothing, but taking care of forty-eight strange children was something else altogether...

Alice Resch was then a young woman in her early thirties. At the time of writing, she lives in her birthplace, Denmark, at the ripe old age of ninety-four.

Menachem: In January 1983, the title of Righteous among the Nations was awarded to Helga Holbeck and Alice Resch, in recognition of their efforts in France during the Holocaust. We, the children of Gurs-Aspet, nominated them. The ceremony was held at the Israel Embassy in Copenhagen. An excerpt from Alice's acceptance speech:

Thank you for the honor you have bestowed on me, and for the beautiful medal. Ms. Holbeck and I don't feel we deserve it, but we thank you and accept it gratefully in the name of the AFSC[15] to whom we owe everything. We have been greatly privileged to work within the framework of this unique organization. Without its financial backing we would not have been able to help... Since the great events of the war years in France we have maintained ties of friendship with the representatives of other organizations, in particular the OSE, and people who were interned in southern France. We met some wonderful people there.

I well recall an old lady in the Recebedou camp near Toulouse. Like thousands of other Jews, she was deported from Germany to France at the beginning of the war and interned in a camp (as we know, some years later they were all sent to death camps in Germany and Poland)... We walked towards the local train station where the freight carriages awaited their human cargo. We saw her

---

15 American Friends Service Committee.

from afar – she was very noticeable in her clean, neat clothes... We expressed our surprise, and she replied: "It is important to keep up one's spirits, and the best way to do so is by maintaining self-respect!" We said "But you're not on the list – you've been hospitalized!" She smiled and said, "I have lived a long and a full life. Now I'm taking the place of a young friend who has all her life before her. No-one will notice that we switched places, all they care about is the numbers..."

I also remember another prisoner, the Rabbi of Gurs. The other inmates thought he was a saint. He was tall and very thin. Our doctor gave him a double ration of porridge every day, but we soon discovered that he always gave it away to someone else...

We are in contact with friends such as these to this day. Many of them now live in Israel... Thank you, Mr. Ambassador, and thank you, my friends in wonderful Israel..."[16]

---

16 Personal communication.

Far from Our Parents

The Orphanage in Aspet

Menachem: Our life in Aspet was palatial in comparison with our miserable existence in Gurs. Ringed by mountains and forested hills, Aspet is situated in a green valley some 650 meters above sea level. The orphanage was a two-story building surrounding a paved courtyard. Several buildings nearby housed the dining room, kitchen, storerooms, and a clinic.

Fred: We were quarantined on our arrival and our heads were shaved (at least, the boys' hair was shaved; we don't remember what they did with the girls). The people in charge hoped by so doing to rid us of the infestation of lice we had brought with us from the camp. It took some time to get rid of all the lice, and in the meantime we children formed symbiotic ties with one another, along the lines of: "You find my lice for me, and I'll help you find yours…" After finding them we became experts in destroying them – balancing them on the tips of our fingernails and squeezing until we heard a satisfying little pop.

We slept in large dormitories, each with about twenty beds. Boys and girls were in separate rooms. Next to each room was a toilet, French style – in other words, a hole in the floor. At the time we were nine and twelve years old; the children ranged in age from six to fifteen. The older girls were put in charge of us, but for the most part we were expected to look after ourselves.

We didn't speak a word of French so we didn't attend the local school. OSE sent the Cohens to try to teach us the rudiments of the French language. They didn't find it easy going – teaching forty-eight children of all ages, who had experienced dreadful traumas, including deportation, separation from their parents, and the daily spectacle of death in the camp. Despite it all, within six months we all spoke some heavily German-accented French and attended the village school.

We were kept apart from the French children, mainly because we couldn't communicate with them. There was also the problem of our peculiar status: we spoke German, the language of the hated enemy, the *sales boches* as they were known, who had defeated the French and occupied their country a mere six months ago. The other kids in the orphanage and the local people didn't always differentiate between the Nazis and the German Jews who had suffered persecution at their hands.

Menachem: In the 1980s, with the help of Uri Landau, one of the Aspet kids who later joined a kibbutz, I managed to track down Jacqueline Sallebert, who took care of us in the orphanage. In 1992, she wrote to me about Mr. Couvot, director of the orphanage:

> Mr. Couvot was responsible for 40 local children who had been abandoned by their mothers (or by both parents) and referred to the orphanage by the welfare authorities. In the course of time many of these children became habitual criminals... It was already difficult for him to feed so many hungry mouths, when suddenly you all appeared... He had to locate farmers willing to sell him – in secret – livestock, flour, milk, and other produce, depending on the time of year. Mr. Couvot was a short man. In order to instill discipline, he often hit his charges... You must bear in mind that before the war it was customary for parents, teachers, and the entire establishment to impose corporal punishment...slaps, ear-pulling and blows to the buttocks were the norm...

Fred: We often went for walks in the pastoral countryside. Wearing the French berets that were popular at the time, we marched along, singing French songs and others with nonsense words: "Oh ligo agri, Oh shama bunga," and so on... The problem was that we marched on empty stomachs. The more daring among us would sneak into the fields and steal whatever we could find, but if we were caught by our minders, the punishment, logically enough, was that we went without a meal.

Menachem: We were always hungry. I stole everything that came my way, at every opportunity. Whenever we went on "nature walks" we formed gangs and plotted our thefts together. While some of us distracted the attention of our minders, I would dive into a nearby field and stuff my mouth and pockets with whatever I could find, depending on the season – beets for cattle, potatoes, pears, cherries, or chestnuts. Usually they were unripe. The important thing was that they filled our rumbling bellies. As an extra precaution I would change my outer garments as soon as I returned from my raid, so even if from a distance someone spotted a boy wearing a red vest – now I was a boy attired in a yellow vest, rolling innocent eyes heavenwards. Believe me, my grandchildren, when I tell you that I know all the tricks!!

One day as a local boy was climbing a cherry tree, the branch snapped. He fell out of the tree and was killed. A large crowd attended his funeral. It was the first time I'd ever been inside a church, and I was curious and scared at the same time.

We played a lot of football. I was an excellent goalkeeper, swooping fearlessly on the ball and on the legs of those kicking the ball... We also played jacks, but most of all we played marbles. We loved playing marbles in the courtyard, close by Jacqueline, who was keeping an eye on us. That way we had a chance to peek up her skirt – or was it Nelly's?

Fred: Mealtimes were always memorable occasions. We were fed in the dining hall. The food I remember best is chickpeas floating in soup. The portions were very meager for us hungry kids. Those who finished first could get a second helping – if there was anything left in the pot, of course. Guess who was a fast eater…?

In a letter, Alice Resch described the daily rations allocated by the Quakers: fifty grams of dried vegetables or thirty grams of rice, fifty grams of noodles, ten grams of oil, ten grams of sugar and concentrated milk, when obtainable. Bless the Quakers!

One item that filled me with revulsion was the boudin – a kind of blood pudding, considered a delicacy. The blood of slaughtered cattle was collected, poured into a shallow dish and baked in the oven. The dish was then sliced and served hot or cold.

Menachem: I didn't find the *boudin* nauseating; on the contrary, it was delicious. For whatever reason, I also enjoyed crunching the stuff they gave us for brushing our teeth. It wasn't a paste but a kind of lump, like a bar of soap. I guess this strange craving arose from the need to replenish the lack of calcium in our diet.

One event that is clearly remembered by everyone who spent time in Aspet was the execution – no other word will do – of cattle, by smashing them with a pickaxe between the horns. To this day I can hear the deep lowing of the animals. We kids stood around, spellbound and almost hypnotized by the blows landing on the head of the tethered animal, as it refused to die. The procedure always ended with the collection of blood for the boudin. That's how we learned about cruelty to animals.

Fred: Laundry was done on the premises. Every item of each child's clothing was marked with a number. The older girls folded the clean laundry and stowed it in our personal cubicles. Before we took our weekly shower, we stood in line to receive clean clothes.

Once a week we were taken down to the cellar. That's where they had the showers. The water was heated in large vats over a wood-burning fire. All the kids had showers on the same day, but only the lucky ones got to shower in hot water. By the time those at the end of the line had their turn, the water was usually cold.

We were expected to take turns with the chores, which included latrine duty. Toilet paper was impossible to obtain so we made do with torn-up newspapers. The doors of the cubicles were not much more than one meter high, and I remember that the walls were sometimes daubed with comma-shaped smears of excrement. We made up our minds to catch the culprit; one of us climbed the wall of a cubicle and kept watch from above. Soon enough a kid came in, sat down, did his business, used his finger to clean himself and then wiped his finger on the wall. That's how the perfect commas kept appearing on the walls. We pounced on him and forced him to clean the toilets. From then on the poor fellow was nicknamed "Virgule" (comma). Children can be very cruel...

Diarrhea and boils were common ailments. The accepted remedy for diarrhea was to chew a piece of medicated charcoal. Fever was treated by "cupping" – the nurse heated a glass beaker by passing a candle flame through it, and then swiftly applied it to the back or chest of the patient – the resulting vacuum drew in the skin and capillaries to stimulate the blood. This treatment was supposed to cure us. If you find this amusing, bear in mind that it was the "alternative medicine" of the time...

Menachem: The doctor made regular visits. He would sit in the office of Mr. Couvot, director of the orphanage, while we passed before him in single file, obediently murmuring "Tout va bien, Docteur" (everything's fine, Doctor). We were only examined when we complained of something.

Fred: Bed-wetting was a most common problem – not at all surprising among children so full of anxiety and insecurity. I was one of them. The embarrassment was acute. We had to pull the mattresses out in the open for all to see. There was no hiding it.

Menachem: Every morning all the wet mattresses were lined up in the yard. The director would arrive, armed with a long cane, and punish the "criminals" in an attempt to cure us.

As Jacqueline wrote, it was customary to impose corporal punishment. When we began to attend school, six months later, we were often made to write 5,000 times (yes, five thousand times!) "I must listen to the teacher and not disturb the class." I would write and write until blood seeped from my fingernails. Anyone who failed to complete his quota was given extra lines. And there was nobody to complain to, no "Society for the Protection of Children." We were supposed to be grateful just for the fact that we were alive.

Fred: It was in Aspet that I first went to the dentist. The treatment did not include anesthetic. I got the standard treatment from the venerable doctor: "Pull it." I was terrified and shrieked.

Menachem: One of the good souls in the orphanage was Nelly, our nurse and social worker, who arrived in March 1942. With Uri's help, we made contact with her in the 1980s. When I began writing this book she sent me an excerpt from her diary, written when she was in Aspet. This is how she described visits to the dentist:

> The clinic of the old dentist faces the marketplace. The stairwell leading to his room is dim and dirty. The wallpaper in the tiny waiting room is peeling… The dentist's surgery isn't any better… A sink in one corner, dusty shelves, an ancient dentist's chair, a spittoon with no running water, a foot-operated drill, its cord continually breaking during treatment; the dentist patches it while his patient waits with mouth wide open. "Close the window, Miss" he says, if an extraction is called for, and then he asks their age. This was very important, because over the age of twelve you were entitled to a local anesthetic. All the kids caught on very quickly, and in no time at all they were all over twelve. The dentist becomes suspicious. The children are alarmed, fearful, terrified! I'm shocked. The children cling to my hand. Between treating one child and the next, the dentist dunks the drill head in a glass of alcohol… Sometimes complications arise, like the time the pulley

of the drill caught on some thread and became tangled in the fly buttons of the old dentist's trousers. He twisted and turned, trying to see what was going on in the region below his fat paunch... finally the pulley snapped, dragging with it one button and a scrap of fabric. I told myself that this time he would definitely change the drill head, but – not a chance! He pulled off the threads and dunked the drill head into the alcohol. "Next..."

Anything at all was better than a visit to the dentist.

Fred: Nelly's diary revealed a great deal about life in Aspet:

September 4, 1942: Most of my time is spent working with children who have no parents. I try to comfort and distract them. Lacking in love, they are deeply grateful for any attention I can provide. Sometimes heartbreaking little notes are left by my door... October 31, 1942: The children are constantly hungry. They grow thinner from week to week. December 6, 1942:... Some of the Jewish children are in my room. It's a long time since they last heard from their parents. They were horrified to hear the stories that a local woman related in their presence. She said that Germans are gassing deported Jews... I could have strangled the stupid woman... Naturally I said it's not true even though I think it is the truth...

Our parents were no longer alive by that time, but of course we had no way of knowing this. Some months earlier, the French government had handed all the people in the concentration camps over to the Germans for their "resettlement" – Auschwitz.

The French Government: Vichy's Role

The Armistice splitting France into two was signed in June 1940 – two-thirds of the country occupied by Germany in the north, the southern third "free." The Vichy Administration under

Marshal Pétain, a World War I hero, had constitutional authority over all of France. In the north, it governed under the eyes of the Germans; in the south, without their presence.

On October 3, 1940, Vichy published the Jewish Statute, adapting Nuremberg-like laws that prohibited Jews from holding posts in public administration or in the army, education, and judicial systems. The following day, Vichy arrested foreign Jews and incarcerated them in camps. This was three weeks before we arrived in Gurs. Vichy required no urging from the Germans to do their bidding.

The Germans' desire to work with the French forced the Germans to implement anti-Jewish measures through Vichy or with its approval. They forced nothing on the French. They made suggestions. The Vichy government went along willingly and even with zeal when German doctrine conformed to its own policy.

Petain even took the precaution of getting advice from the Vatican on the Jewish measures. Vichy's ambassador to the Vatican reported: "Never has anything been said to me in the Vatican that might suggest, on the part of the Holy See, criticism or disapproval of the legislation in question."[17]

This is, of course, a whole other story, in contrast with the many heroic French clergymen and nuns who saved thousands. See the recently published book *Hitler's Pope*.[18]

Using methods already well-proven in Germany, Eichmann's representative in France, Theodor Dannecker, established a three-step process for dealing with the Jews. In coordination with the French police, he conducted a census of all Jews; this was followed by laws registering Jewish businesses with the intent of taking them over. Lastly, they imposed nighttime curfews and prohibited any change of domicile. This way, they could lay their hands on the Jews when the time was right.

---

17 Report by Ambassador Bernard to the Vatican on the Jewish legislation, September 1941.
18 John Cornwall, *Hitler's Pope*, New York 1999.

This was followed by the establishment within the Vichy government of the General Commissariat for Jewish Affairs in March 1941, after lengthy discussions between the Germans and Vichy. The Petain government was willing to organize a central body to deal with the "Jewish Question" (sound familiar?) according to the wishes of the German military authority, because it feared that Vichy would not get its share of confiscated Jewish property in the north. How's that for motivation?

Xavier Vallat was appointed Commissioner. He was not an antisemite in the Nazi mold, and did not advocate the Final Solution. His views were in line with his malleable Vichy bosses, who wanted to discriminate against Jews, but not kill them. Vallat first acted against foreign Jews because of Pétain's insistence that French Jews, particularly those who had served in the First World War or those *vielle souche* families who had lived in France for centuries, should not be harmed.

During that time, we forty-eight kids continued living in Aspet, unaware of the growing danger that threatened to engulf us. During that entire period we continued to correspond with our parents and other family members.

Last Letters

Fred: We were getting used to our new environment – did we have any choice? We had to learn a new language, adjust to living with other children, and for the first time in our lives, we were far away from our parents. It's important to emphasize that during this time we corresponded with them regularly. We were always waiting for the mailman. The first letter reached us after a week.

Menachem: How is it that we still have these letters? On July 19, 1959, a large envelope arrived from Fred, containing some forty letters written to us by our parents and other people in the camps. He included a letter of his own:

> I am enclosing letters from our parents. I don't know why I kept them all these years... I considered burning them, but on second thought I decided to send them on to you because they belong to you as well. Do with them what you will.

Until then I was not aware of the existence of the letters. I'd forgotten that we wrote to each other. Fred kept them with him throughout his wanderings.

When they arrived I put them away in a drawer – unread! At the time, neither of us was capable, in a psychological sense, of looking back and analyzing our traumatic past history. We forced ourselves to forget; we suppressed it, neither of us wanted to remember. Fred sent the letters away, out of his sight, and I stuffed them into a drawer. For many years, I did not let the past catch me unawares. I re-read the letters for the first time in the 1970s, some thirty years after the events took place. Somehow the reading refreshed my memory, and I had sudden brief glimpses and flashes of recall – waiting for the mailman at his usual spot, the joy when we received a letter and the disappointment when our names weren't called.

The first letter is dated March 1, 1941, and the last one – August 10, 1942. Most of them were written by our parents, particularly Mother, but we also received mail from other members of the family. Sometimes the letters included remarks and good wishes from our uncles, neighbors, and acquaintances. From the letters, it appears that parcels were also mailed between us. Most of them were sent from the Rivesaltes camp where our parents were taken, some from Gurs, and a few from other places.

The letters are in very cramped writing, because they were all censored. They deal mainly with everyday life in the camp, the inadequate food, incessant hunger, their concern for us, their children, and their conviction that they did the right thing by sending us away. Our parents write about the past, their longings for their former life, and their hope that we would be reunited in the future. And between the lines we learn a great deal about our parents and ourselves, how they coped with the great gap in distance and years that yawned between us. It is remarkable how much they involved us – children not yet thirteen years old – in their daily lives, their worries and their concerns, especially when we consider they had no idea they were writing for posterity.

We have tried to remain faithful to the original text. These, the last words of those who perished, are very precious to us.

[1]

Gurs Camp, 1st March 1941
Dear children,

We were very happy to receive your first letter and we are pleased things are going well in Aspet. Did you manage to see me? When the truck passed, I was standing on the wooden bridge waving goodbye. Everything happened so fast. Inge[19] is in hospital with whooping cough. Grandmother is still in the clinic.

The transport will leave for Rivesaltes[20] on March 10th.

We don't know whether we will be included. They say only families with children will be moved. Did you get some goodies on [...]? What do they give you to eat? How do you spend your time?

Best wishes and kisses, Mother

Dear Manfred and Heinz,

We were happy to hear from you, and to know you are healthy and well looked after. I don't know when we will leave. I hope you will write us a long and detailed letter. Manfred and Heinz, be good boys. Andrée Salomon says you are good boys. Pay attention in school, so you will learn.

Best wishes and kisses, Father

---

19 Inge (Ingrid) was the daughter of Moritz (Father's brother) and Alma. At some point she was removed from Gurs and hidden until after the war by a Catholic family, the Eisenreichs. In 1995, the family was honored by Yad Vashem as Righteous among the Nations. After the war, Ingrid was located by her uncles in America, who took her in, and today she lives in San Diego, California.

20 Rivesaltes concentration camp was situated some ten kilometers north of Perpignan, not far from the Mediterranean seashore. Originally intended as a military camp when it was built in 1938, it was a desolate and barren place, strewn with rocks and exposed to biting winds. The camp extended over an area of 600 hectares and contained ISO concrete and asbestos barracks arranged in 10 blocks. On December 10, 1940, this military camp became a concentration camp intended for 17,000-18,000 people. Our parents were transported to Rivesaltes two weeks after we were separated.

Dear children,

We were very happy to receive your letter. Inge is still in hospital, but she is much better. I'm pleased you are well and happy. Keep well and write us good news.

> Regards and kisses from Aunt Alma, Inge and Uncle Moritz

Dear Manfred and Heinz,

I would like to add a few words to your mother's letter. I wish you well from the bottom of my heart and hope we will meet again in this life. Best wishes from far away; I am with you in prayer.

> Irma Amelda Ohbert[21]

Dear Manfred and Heinz,

I also send you regards. Be well and behave. We bless you with all our hearts.

> Eugen and Gerda[22]

Dear Manfred and Heinz,

God's blessings on you both. Hoping you are well and you have good [...]. May God continue to help you. Pray to Him devoutly. I wish you all the best and hope we will meet again soon.

> Heartfelt wishes from your friend Thea

---

21 Irma is also mentioned in later letters as "deaf Irma." We don't remember her. She was probably one of the neighbors in the barracks.
22 The Ledermann couple, who were deported from Hoffenheim, perished in Auschwitz.

[2]

Rivesaltes, 14th March 1941
Dear children,

You will no doubt be surprised to read that we are no longer in
Gurs. Since 11th March we have been in Rivesaltes. Grandmother
and Uncle Emanuel are still there [in Gurs]. Dear Manfred and
Heinz – are you already going to school? I'm sure it's beautiful
where you are, be happy you are there. I hope you have settled
down. Dear Manfred – you are the eldest, look after Heinz and
make sure he learns something. Pay attention to your teachers
and be good boys. Kisses from your Father. The address is:

Karl Mayer
Baraque 24, îlot F
Centre d'hebergement de Rivesaltes

Mother is in a different block. I have visited her already. She's
writing to you. Did you receive her letter? Write soon. Manfred,
don't lose the stamps.

[3]

Rivesaltes, 18th March 1941
Dear children,

How are you? I hope everything is well. Thank God, everything
is fine here as well. Did you receive the letter I sent before we left
Gurs? I waited to hear from you – but in vain. Other children who
left have already written to their parents. The children write that
they are happy. A children's home is a children's home, and a camp
is a camp… We traveled over the bridge by train.[23] The sea stretches
on both sides of the bridge. Aunt Alma and Irma are still in Gurs.

---

23 From Gurs to Rivesaltes.

Here the barracks are made of stone with windows. In our barrack the beds are arranged on two levels. The older women sleep on the bottom bunks and the younger women on top, because you have to climb up. I sleep on top, and I also have room for my suitcase. The small children sleep with their mothers because there is no children's barrack or school. Do you go to school? It hasn't rained since we arrived, and there aren't any wells, so we do our laundry in the washrooms. Twice a day we get hot water in the kitchen. Father started working on Monday so he gets a little extra.

I want to send a birthday present for Heinz. Did you get something from your uncle? Should I send your vests and Heinz's light blue trousers?

Heinz, for your ninth birthday I wish you health. Be a good and obedient boy. You should also write. Are you pleased with the place? They say it is beautiful in Aspet, where you are. Do you have a garden?

Write soon. Best wishes and kisses from your loving Mother

Dear Manfred and Heinz,

Why don't you write? I hope you are feeling well. I am fine. Other children have already written lovely letters. Happy birthday Heinz, I hope you are a good boy. Write us a long letter.

All the best from your Father

[4]

24th March 1941
Dear children,

Manfred, we received the two letters and the postcard and they made us very happy. We were pleased to read that you are healthy and pleased with the place. Heinz, why don't you write? You must also write to us. What do you do all day? Are you learning? Be careful not to catch cold. Is the weather stormy? The winds are very strong here. We aren't far from the sea, the camp is only 7 kilometers away. The train crossed the sea on the way here. The camp is big – 28 kilometers. We can visit the men's barracks every day between 9-11 and 2-6 in the afternoon.

Father is working on the roads and he gets an extra piece of bread and a little [...]. The roads are full of stones.

We haven't yet received a package from you. Find out if it was sent to us. We can't buy anything in the canteen except dry dates, and they are very expensive. Did you receive a parcel from your uncle? I heard that everything is distributed to the children. I can't get hold of hangers, toothpaste, or a lock. I will try to get a permit to travel to the village of Rivesaltes. It's about one hour away. Two weeks ago I wrote to your grandmother and uncle Emanuel, but I haven't received a reply. Eugen and Moritz and their families haven't arrived yet. The third transport from Gurs is expected tomorrow.

Mr. Rosenberg[24] wanted to bring you and Leo back because he thought you weren't happy there, but a children's home is different from a camp. I heard that Mrs. Cohen[25] from Gurs will be coming to you. Is that true?

I'm fairly happy here, after the endless rain in Gurs. Last night we were given a bowl of pea soup and a bowl of vegetable soup.

For your birthday, Heinz, I've started to knit you a sleeveless vest from the gray wool in Gurs. Yesterday I was in Rivesaltes village. It was nice. I bought some things, but before I send them I want to finish the vest. Tell Heinz to write. All the best,

Kisses from your Mother

---

24 Mr. Rosenberg from Bruchsahl was deported from Baden to Gurs. He was on good terms with our parents. **Menachem:** His son, Leo Rosenberg, was a good friend of mine. He was with us in Aspet and he was smuggled into Switzerland with me. After the war, he made his way to England, where he now lives.

25 She and her husband were appointed by OSE to teach us French in Aspet.

[5]

Rivesaltes, 20th April 1941
Dear Manfred and Heinz,

Today I am beginning to write letters. I hope you are well. Thank
God we are too. We were very pleased to receive your letters, and
especially to know that you're happy where you are. Be glad you
are there. This week a package will be sent. Mother is knitting
a vest for Heinz and she lengthened Manfred's. Share the other
things, don't fight over them. We haven't received anything from
the United States. Manfred, be frugal with the stamps. What's
news with you? Write soon.

All the best from your Father. Tell Heinz to write.

Dear children,

We finally received your letter and it made us very happy,
especially to know that you are well and happy where you are.
The men are in the same block with us – block B – but in separate
barracks. Which tooth of Heinz's was extracted? Was it a milk
tooth? [...] Did you have a Seder? I would have sent you the
things I bought in Rivesaltes village 3-4 weeks ago: shoe polish,
a lock, and toothpaste, but I wanted to finish the vest for Heinz
and to lengthen yours, Manfred, before I sent the parcel. I would
have finished a long time ago, but I spent the whole week cleaning
vegetables in the kitchen. For working in the kitchen they give
you extra soup. Father is working on the roads. Uncle Emanuel
wrote, and Uncle Moritz also wrote two letters. Aunt Alma didn't
reply to my letter, you didn't need to write to her!

Are the trees in bloom over there? There are no trees here.

Manfred, do you still need the coat? It is very expensive to
send large packages. You didn't reply to the questions in my last
letter. There's no news here. The men are living in the same block
as the women. They can visit their wives from 9 in the morning

until 8 in the evening, but Father works every day from 8 in the morning until 5 in the evening. It seems you have good food, do you get meat every day? Write soon. Best regards to Leo and Hugo Schiller.[26] Mr. Rosenberg has a relative in Aspet. His name is Frei, you should visit him.

Kisses from your Mother

[6]

Rivesaltes, [22th] April 1941
Dear children,

We were very pleased with your letter. Now we know you are well and we are too. Manfred and Heinz, we write to you once a week, and that will have to do. How much can we write? Manfred, you should write along the length of the page, not the width, and two pages at most. This week you will receive the letter. Manfred, why are you annoyed when […]? We will write to you every week, you can count on it.

All the best and kisses from your Father

My dear children,

We received your letter, and we gather you are happy. We are also healthy, at least. I always say: "Even lengthy suffering ends well." Tomorrow I will send the package: two pairs of trousers, toothpaste, shoe polish, a toothbrush, the two vests of course, and something to nibble on. Dear Heinz, I was so sorry to read that you had a toothache. I have also had toothache for the past few days, so I know how it feels. We have vegetable soup every day, usually carrot soup. Sometimes I do other people's laundry, but

26 He was sent with us to Aspet, and in 1941, OSE and the Quakers arranged for him to be sent to the United States.

I don't have as many customers as I had in Gurs. Give Leo and Hugo some of the sweets. Do Ernst and Richard Weilheimer[27] share a room with Heinz?

Manfred, send me the address of Dr. Franck from Limoges. He is related to Richard and Ernst and he released their grandmother. He would know the whereabouts of Henriette Sandler from Hoffenheim.[28] Have you visited Mr. Frei in Aspet?

The Seder was held in the barrack we use as a synagogue. It was warm last week but now it's cold again. This week there was only nougat to be had in the canteen. Your diarrhea must have been terrible. Please God it's over. Can't you find any shoe polish in Aspet? What about toothpaste? Who darns your socks? Do you have darning thread? I am enclosing a little darning thread with this letter.

Regards to Hugo and Leo.
Best wishes and kisses from your Mother.

[7]

[15th] May 1941
Dearest children,

I hope you received the letter and parcel. Your letter made us very happy. I didn't know that you, Heinzl, also know how to write such lovely big letters. Manfred, why do you write so little? Please write along the length of the page, not the width [a censor's note is attached, pointing out that letters may not exceed two pages]. Manfred, why do you need a cap? You had a new black cap when you left – did you lose it? The one I sent is for Heinz, because he doesn't have a good one. Please, boys, don't fight over it. You

---

27 Ernst and Richard Weilheimer were sent with us to Aspet. They were both sent to the United States in 1941 (together with Hugo) and survived.

28 Henriette Sandler née Ledermann moved to France before the war.

didn't mention whether you have gained weight. What about a photograph? Send us one when you can. Uncle Emanuel wrote that Grandmother is still in the clinic. Father isn't [working] in the kitchen yet. He repairs roads. I go to the kitchen each morning at 6 to clean vegetables: carrots and beets for soup. It suddenly turned cold. Today is Sunday, it's raining. The roads here are better than at Gurs. Did Mr. and Mrs. Cohen leave Aspet? Who is with you now? Theo says he wrote to you. He wants to join you, but it's impossible. Write to us and describe what you found in the parcel. Did you find the toothbrush? Does Heinz still need the padlock? I don't know where to find one. Did you learn French already? Here in the kitchen one can learn a little Spanish and French, because only Spanish people work here.

Uncle Emanuel has been working in the kitchen in Gurs for the past two weeks.

That's all for today, all the best and kisses from your Mother
[...]²⁹

[8]

4th June 1941
Dearest children,

We received your letter and were especially pleased to know you are well and happy there. Is there a school? Manfred, you wrote very little. My letter should have reached you a long time ago, but it came back because it was too big. How did you celebrate the holiday?³⁰ Did you have a prayer service? We held services outside on Sunday because the weather was nice, and inside the hut on Monday because it was raining. On Sunday I worked in the kitchen as usual, peeling carrots and preparing vegetables for

---

29 We were unable to decipher an enclosure sent with this letter.
30 Judging by the date, the reference was to Shavuoth (Pentecost).

soup. What food do they give you? Do you know whether the Limoges children went to America? You aren't on the list, are you? You didn't mention whether the vests were in the parcel. Heinz, do they fit? Don't lose them. I spoke to Theo. He sent you a letter a few weeks ago, didn't you get it? Look after the new cap, wear it only on weekends. I'm pleased to hear that you have gained weight. I have a very modern figure now! Spring has passed. How time flies – what will become of us? I miss the forest. Do you remember our walks in the forest, two to four hours walking to Neidenstein? When the beautiful castle came into view, we recited the poem "Welcome to the sunshine" Do you remember when we went to Steinsfurt?

Perhaps it's better this way? Is it beautiful in Aspet? That's all for today.

All the best and kisses from all my heart, your Mother

My dear children,

We were happy to read your letter because we could see you are well and healthy. We are too. We are specially pleased to know you are happy there. Be good boys. Manfred, you asked about your English book – we don't have it here, you know how it was. We haven't yet heard from […]. I'll write him again. We had a letter from Uncle Emanuel and Grandmother. They're well. Write soon.

All the best and kisses from your Father

[9]

6th June 1941
My dearest children,

I hope you are well, that's the most important thing. We are fine. Is it hot where you are? The last few days have been very hot, particularly in the mornings, but the afternoons are chilly. Today the weather is stormy. We received your letter yesterday and it made us very happy. What kind of work are you doing in the fields? You are right, Manfred, I would also have enjoyed working in the field or a garden, but what can we do? Today I began work before 5:30 in the morning, cleaning vegetables for the soup. There are four kitchens: one for the children, one for the women and two for the men. There is also a kosher kitchen. I work in the children's kitchen. Father still works on road repair. Write me your daily menu. What vegetables do they give you? Do they add flour? Let me know whether the vests were in the parcel. Did you like them? I embroidered them with your initials. This week I did some laundry for other people, because we don't have any money. We haven't heard from Aunt Elsa or from America. I wrote again, this time in English. Manfred, I don't have an English textbook and I don't have any money to buy one. I must find someone who can get a padlock from Perpignan.[31] They only issue travel permits to people who need medical attention or to visit someone who is sick in hospital.

You are beginning to study early for your bar mitzvah, Manfred. Who knows where you will be then? You didn't sign up for America? Do you think they'll put you onto a transport? Hanna Levy and Liesl Herman are in my barrack. They are [related to] Fred Lange, who worked with Father in the kitchen in Gurs. I have become thin, probably from constantly climbing up to the top bunk each day. Have you ever seen a bunk bed? Did you get anything from the large parcel that Leo received? Does Heinz still have the three pairs of boots? Why does he write that he's still wearing the halfboots? He said they were small when we still lived at home. He must take care not to ruin his feet. Reply soon.

Kisses from your Mother

---

31 A town near Rivesaltes.

[10]

Rivesaltes, 18th June 1941
My dear children,

We are pleased to know you are healthy and happy. What work are you doing in the fields? Theo wrote a long letter to you some time ago, but his grandfather, who is in barrack no. 29, keeps it in his pocket. I see that you have good food. We don't get any vegetable dishes apart from soup – it's understandable, after all, there are thousands of people here. I am pleased the vests fit and you like the embroidered initials. I work in the kitchen every day from 6 in the morning to 11:30, and for this I get an extra portion of soup. Do you remember how you refused the fish oil at home?! How much weight have you gained?

I didn't get any mail from Gurs for my birthday.[32] Father gave me a bottle of wine. Now fruit and vegetables are available in the canteen. Unfortunately I have no money apart from the few francs I earn for the laundering. We don't get letters or parcels from anyone, not even from Aunt Elsa, even though I wrote to her in English several times. Did you speak to Rabbi Dr. Kappel[33] about the English [text] book? You also, Heinzl, thank you for what you wrote. Give my regards to Richard, Ernst, Leo and

---

32 Mother was born on June 18, 1898.
33 At the outbreak of the Second World War, Dr. Kappel was drafted to the French Army as military chaplain. On his discharge he was appointed assistant rabbi in the detention camps in southern France, working tirelessly for the welfare of the inmates. At the same time, he joined the underground Organization of Fighting Jews as chaplain with the rank of sergeant. From 1946-1949, he was involved in organizing Haganah units in North Africa, and in 1954 he made aliyah (immigrated to Israel) and worked at the Ministry of Foreign Affairs. He was Israel's ambassador in Athens and Central America from 1960 to 1968. Menachem met him for the first time in the 1970s at the synagogue they both attended.

Hugo. Heinz, I see you are learning French very well; I have also learned a bit – from the Spanish people who work in the kitchen.

For today, all the best and kisses from your Mother Dear Manfred and Heinz,

Hoping you are well, I am fine. It's midsummer and very hot. In my next letter I'll write about the name for your bar mitzvah. There's still time. That all for now, write soon.

                                        All the best from your Father

[11]

Rivesaltes, 30th June 1941
My beloved children,

We received your two letters and of course they made us very happy. I thought I wrote to you, but I must have forgotten in the midst of my concerns. My days are very busy in addition to the work in the kitchen. A week ago I did night duty twice in the clinic. I receive half a liter of milk and a slice of bread for doing this work (from 8 at night until 7:30 in the morning), and then I do laundry to earn some money, because nobody sends us parcels.

Father is now working in the stables, feeding the horses. They are used for transportation in the camp. It's very hot here, even inside the stone barracks. Do you also have a lot of flies and mosquitoes? Don't forget to wear hats when you're out in the hot sun. Do you have good food? What are the other children doing? I thought you would send us a photograph. I would be happy to send you some money to take a picture. Heinz, why didn't you write in the last letter? Theo is in Block B, barrack no. 29. Men and women are in the same block.

Be well, may God watch over you. Trust in Him and ask Him to keep you healthy, that's the main thing.

                For today all the best, from your Mother who loves you

Dear Manfred and Heinz,

Why didn't you write this week? We usually receive a letter every week, so we are concerned. I hope you are feeling well, we are too. Mother already wrote to you that now I'm working in a new place – with horses. I'm pleased to know you are happy. When you go outside wear a hat. Nothing new here. Tell Heinz he should also write. Manfred, write on the length of the page.

Hugs from all my heart and kisses, your Father

[12]

Rivesaltes, 30th July 1941
Dearest children,

This letter has been waiting for eight days, because I didn't have a stamp. Yesterday your letter arrived. I'm glad you are well and happy. I am so pleased you are there and not here. On Saturday two weeks ago Father was taken with more than 200 men to work somewhere. Until now I haven't heard from him. When I know his address I'll send it to you.[34] Maybe Uncle Emanuel and Uncle Moritz were sent as well? I haven't heard from Grandmother or from Aunt Elsa. I don't understand why she doesn't reply. Have you heard from Helmut?[35] You asked what vegetables they give

---

34 Father and most of the healthy men in Rivesaltes were taken to build the Atlantic Wall in the vicinity of the harbor town of Brest in western France. This was a system of fortifications built by the Germans in the summer of 1941 along the French and Belgian shoreline opposite the coast of England. These fortifications were designed and constructed by an engineer, Fritz Todt, using thousands of forced laborers. Father was sent back to Rivesaltes six weeks later.

35 Helmut, Aunt Elsa's son, was held in Paderborn camp in Germany. He was killed in Auschwitz on March 1, 1943.

us? Nothing but carrots and beets for soup. What vegetables do you get? I spoke to Mrs. Wildmann about your inoculations. You had three, not four. I thought you would send a photograph of yourselves.

Now, about your Jewish names: Manfred is Maier bar Kalonymous, and Heinz is Menachem bar Kalonymous. Write them down. Today it is very stormy and difficult to write. The last few weeks have been very hot. Do you still have the clothes you took with you? I'm worried because you keep writing about a padlock. I'll try to get a padlock for you but it costs 15-20 francs, and that's a lot of money when you only get a few centimes for laundry. Are the shoes I gave Heinz small for him or did they break? Manfred, what about your brown Sabbath shoes? And what of your high orthopedic shoes? It's nice that there's a cattle fair, you can see cows. Write and tell us whether you can send us a few kilograms of potatoes. If you can, I'll send you money. I signed up for a course to learn French, two evenings a week. It's held in the young people's clubhouse where they have lectures, games, and discussions.

That's all for today, kisses from your Mother who loves you

[13]

Rivesaltes, [...] August 1941
Dearest children,

We were very happy to receive your letter. I was especially happy to read that you are well, because that's really the most important thing. Did you get the letter where I wrote that Father was taken from here with more than 100 other men? Three weeks have passed and I still haven't heard from him. They say they were taken to work. What do you say to this? If only we knew where they were.

A letter arrived from Aunt Elsa. She says she has written before, and she wrote to you as well. She doesn't mention sending a parcel. We haven't received a parcel from you. Miss Salomon[36] was here, she'll come again. Yesterday I received a letter from the uncle in Gurs, he wrote that he received a letter from you. He has been in the clinic for four weeks now, because a pot of boiling soup spilt on his leg. Something always happens! If only I heard from Father. I don't hear anything from the uncle here. Do you have Helmut's address? I sent regards to Theo. Who sends you parcels? It's terrible that Mrs. Weilheimer[37] died – now you can see how good it is to have a mother. Please give my condolences to Ernst and Richard. Best regards to Leo. What do you get to eat? Do you get cooked meals like you had at home? We get watery vegetable soup, sometimes with potatoes.

Heinzlein wrote a long letter this time. He already knows how to write like a real gentleman. I wish I could visit you, but I don't have any money. Someone from here spent eight days over there and liked the place very much. I am enclosing three stamps. Manfred, I don't know how long it takes for mail to arrive, 6-8 days? Lately I have been suffering quite badly from diarrhea. In the photograph you sent your face looks thin, Manfred, and is Heinz's neck swollen?

Regards and kisses from your Mother, who loves you with all her heart

They just brought your passport photos, you look well. Why do you need them? Are you going away?

---

36 Andree Salomon of OSE, who removed us from Gurs to Aspet.
37 The mother of Ernst and Richard, who were with us in Aspet. They are frequently mentioned in our parents' letters.

[14]

Brest, 16th August 1941[38]
Dear Manfred and Heinz,

I assume you have heard from Mother and I hope you are both well, so am I.

Dear Manfred and Heinz – don't worry about me. It's enough that I worry about you.

My dear children, I have only one small request, it's not much: Manfred, look after Heinz, make sure nothing happens to him, you are his big brother. Learn well in school and behave yourselves. This is my request. My dear children, do what I ask, so I won't have to worry about you all the time.

Write to Mother and give her my regards. Write soon.

Best wishes and kisses from your Father
Regards to my son Horst Wallenstein[39]

[15]

Aspet, 10th September 1941[40]

Dear Father, we received your postcard so we know you arrived safely. Where do you sleep? What work are you doing?

---

38 Father managed to send us this postcard while he was in Brest building the Atlantic Wall. His overwhelming despair cries out from every line. I view these words as a kind of last will and testament. On September 10, 1941, we wrote to him in Brest (letter no. 15), but our letter was returned because the same day he was sent back to Rivesaltes.

39 This line was written by the father of one of the Aspet children. We don't remember him.

40 This letter was sent to Father in Brest. The letter never reached him because he was sent back to Rivesaltes.

I gave regards to Horst Wallenstein. How's the food? My Rosh Hashanah wish is that next year we will all be together. Are you allowed to write letters? Your wishes came true. Lots of love and kisses, Manfred.

Manfred sends regards. Please give regards to Mr. Wallenstein from his son Horst.[41]

Dear Father, we received your postcard and saw you are well. I'm fine. Best wishes for Rosh Hashana. You don't have to worry about us, we're fine.

Lots of love and kisses, Heinz

[16]

Rivesaltes, 11th September 1941

My dear children, I am sure you are surprised that I'm writing to you from here. We returned on September 10th. We must thank God. Are you well? Dear Manfred and Heinz, did you receive the postcard I sent you? I thought about you a lot. Be happy that you are where you are. Write soon.

All the best and kisses from your Father

My dear children,

Your letter arrived yesterday. It made me very happy, especially to know you are well and healthy. You had an interesting and enjoyable Sunday. Yesterday, Tuesday, they suddenly announced that the men were back. I couldn't believe it... The journey took eight days! Father is now living in block F, because he's working

---

41 This line was written in different handwriting – it is the reply of our
   friend in Aspet to his father.

in the stables again. He feeds the horses. The stables are in F. They use the horses to transport waste from the barracks and the kitchen. The toilets are emptied by machine. Now Father gets paid something for the work.

I haven't written yet to OSE. Do you want to go to America?[42] Should we apply for ourselves as well? It's already 11 months since we left home. Such a long time! I am learning French and English. On Sundays we have concerts – violin recitals and singing. This week, after I heard from Father, I went for the first time. They had good food, but they had to haul cement blocks for eight days, twelve hours at night and then in the daytime, over and over. Now I'm happy because Father is back. He is permitted to come here at 5:30 but they must be back in block F by 8:30. When he is here I cook something. Today I made bread balls from my bread ration and cooked them in garlic sauce. Father said they were tasty. Sometimes I cook Schnitznöfee with two or three pears in the little stove. Two weeks ago I heard from Mrs. Hirsch Ladenburg that Jakob Hirsch and his sisters were in a transport. Also Hermannel Rosenfeld. The Hirsch family were in Marseilles when the children sailed on the ship. It was very hard for their mother to part from them. For the first time I have received a letter from Ludwig Kaufmann.[43] Laupertheimer asked him for our address, finally we've heard from them. They sent Ludwig a little money for us, we'll know what to do with it.

---

42 At the beginning of the war, America agreed, under pressure, to take in a number of Jewish children. Beginning in 1941, several hundred entry permits for healthy children under the age of 16 were issued. With the help of the OSE, three groups of children set sail from Marseilles, but the operation was halted when the Allies invaded North Africa on November 11, 1942, and contact was severed with the United States. The last group departed very close to this date, leaving one thousand unused permits that had been allocated in the summer of 1942.

43 Apparently a relative of ours, since our maternal grandmother was a Kaufmann.

The canteen has fruit, tomatoes and other vegetables. Yesterday I wrote to Gurs about your vaccination card. Yesterday all the children here were vaccinated.

All the best and kisses from your Mother

[17]

Rivesaltes, 8th November 1941
My dearest children,

Yesterday we received your letter, and thank God you are well. Look after yourselves in the cold weather and dress warmly. Do you still have the warm socks? Does Heinz's vest still fit him? I imagine the dark blue suit with red is small on him by now. Why does Heinz always write that he has to stay inside because he has no shoes? I gave him three pairs of high-topped shoes and one pair of galoshes – where did they all disappear to? It's a pity I have no wool – I would knit socks for you. If only we had taken the vests and woolen socks with us from home. Do they give you warm clothes? Should I send the blue winter coat? We bought a padlock for Heinz.

Manfred, I don't know what to advise you about Heinz. Ask if it is permitted to take your brother.[44] I think it's better for you to remain together than to have one here and one there. I heard from OSE that someone will come to Aspet soon to arrange categories of travel to America. Miss Salomon is here now. She says she'll be going to Aspet soon. I want to send you something, but there are freezing winds outside and it's impossible to get to the post office because it's far away in another block. Also, I have a swollen cheek so they must remove an abscessed tooth. If it's not one thing it's another… I must look after myself because

---

44 There was a possibility of going to America, but from the letters it appears that only Fred's name appeared on the list of those who were issued permits.

I keep getting diarrhea. A letter arrived from Aunt Elsa, dated 15th August. She says she received one letter from us in August, but we wrote to her several times!! Theo left. Now he works in a restaurant. Kurt Altstadter has also left. I don't know whether he went to an institution or somewhere else. Father is still working in the military camp with toilet machinery. He gets a little extra bread and soup. Uncle Emanuel sent your vaccination cards from Gurs. Should I send them to you? Just don't lose them. Do you have stoves for heating? There is no heat here. The barrack is large, big enough for ninety or a hundred people. Did you receive the last stamps I sent you? Manfred, after thinking it over again, perhaps you can take Heinz with you. I think it's preferable that you should be together.

From now on you must write a number next to the name. My number is: 5273.

> Be well, kisses from your Mother
> Sender: Mathilde Mayer 5273
> Camp de Rivesaltes
> Centre d'hébergement
> Baraque 20, îlot B

[18]

Rivesaltes, 20th November 1941
My beloved children,

We received your letter and see that you are healthy, thank God. Father is also well. I must take care of myself because I get diarrhea very easily.[45] What do you get to eat? What has Heinz done with all the shoes I gave him – three pairs of high-topped shoes, half shoes and a pair of wooden clogs? If the shoes are small on him, send them here and I'll sell them. How can it be that you don't have boots? What is your shoe size? How are your

---

45 The next few words were erased by the censor.

socks, I'm sure they're torn by now?! They aren't available here. The last time they asked what you needed you should have said you need shoes and socks. Perhaps Heinz can still travel with you? I can't judge from here. Miss Salomon from OSE was here a few weeks ago. She said she would go to Aspet to see about the journey to America. I think you will soon be getting new supervisors, and then you will go to school again. Why do they change so often? We can learn English once a week. The teacher is Mrs. Cohen. She was with you in Gurs. Father's Jewish name is Kalonymous bar Aharon, and we are "Israel." The storm has just ended, but it may return tomorrow. A biting wind penetrates the roof and makes its way to me, because I sleep on the top bunk on a wooden pallet. The floor below is made of concrete, and we have no heaters yet. They haven't taken out my tooth yet, I'm afraid of the extraction. Yesterday in the evening I went to a concert. The conductor was Alfred Kalm. It was nice. I went so I could think of other things.

Uncle Moritz is working in the kitchen in Gurs. I wrote to Uncle Emanuel. Yesterday I received a letter from Seppel[46] – he asks about the watch. He needs it and asks whether you sold it. I wrote to Aunt Elsa. Thank God, I was not vaccinated because I have my vaccination card from Gurs. Father lives in block F in the workers' barrack. He comes to visit each evening between 6 and 7:30. I will put the vaccination cards in the parcel together with two pairs of slippers, a coat, a belt, one cup, 2 cubes of chocolate, 2 nougats, handkerchiefs, writing paper, and socks for school. How much do you weigh, Heinz? We have not been weighed. Regards to Leo, Ernst and Richard. Send me the shoes that are too small for you, perhaps I can exchange them.[47]

All the best and kisses from your Mother who loves you

---

46 Yosef Scherer, a family member who lived in Sinsheim, near HofTenheim. He was deported with us and sent to Gurs.
47 The next words were erased by the censor.

[19]

Rivesaltes, 10th December 1941
My dear children,

We received your letters together with the Hanukkah gifts, and
we know you are feeling well. Thank God we are also well. My
diarrhea is getting better. Who knitted the handkerchief holders?
They made me very happy. Father was also very pleased with
the cutlery holder. Did you receive the vaccination cards? Don't
lose them. I sent you 30 francs so Mr. Wildstrom[48] would send
us a parcel. Mrs. Kollmann paid 30 francs and received a parcel
from him with fruit, onions and chestnuts. If at all possible,
I desperately need onions, garlic and Muscat grapes. I hope
the socks and shoes fit. I would like to knit caps for you – but
I don't have wool. Ask Mr. Wildstrom if he can... I would be very
grateful to him. We talked to Dr. Basnitzky[49] about America – we
don't know anything. I am enclosing a permit. Now that I'm
feeling better, I've started taking in laundry again to earn money.
We only received money from America once. We had a letter from
Aunt Alma and Uncle Emanuel from Gurs. Eugen[50] added a few
lines. Gerdie never writes. Father got the belts for you.

All the best, Mother

Dear children,

I hope you are feeling well, thank God we are too. I hope
you received the parcel and the money. Perhaps you can send
something. Dear Manfred and Heinz, I have nothing to tell you,

---

48   A Jewish refugee hiding in the village of Aspet.
49   The father of George, one of the Aspet children. Menachem located
     George in the 1970s in Bet Nekofa near Jerusalem.
50   Eugen Ledermann and his wife Gerdie were deported from
     Hoffenheim. They both perished in Auschwitz.

Mother wrote everything. The padlock is in the pocket of the coat, don't lose it. The belts match. Write soon.

All the best and kisses from your Father

[20]

Rivesaltes, 26th January 1942
My dear children,

I hope you received the letter from last week. For the past 14 days I have been working in the kindergarten. I light the stove, clean the classrooms and wash the dishes. The children get milk at 10 and at noon – porridge. I am going to write to Dr Kappel. I already wrote to him once, but the address was wrong. It's probably too late. Today I went to Dr. Basnitzky and read the beautiful compositions you each wrote.

It appears to me that you argue too much, please don't. It seems that Richard receives lots of parcels, it that correct? Perhaps from Dr. Frank. That's nice. I see that with various people in my barrack like Irma Heumann from Neidenstein, the mother of Liesel. Liesel also left this week. She moved to a children's home. Irene Kayem also went to an institution two weeks ago. This week, for the first time, we had potato soup or rice soup for a change. I don't have time anymore for my French and English lessons. I'm happy if I manage to do the laundry and mend the clothes. I work in the kindergarten every day from 5:30 to 11:30 and in the afternoon from 2:30 to 6:00. The buildings here are made of stone with cement floors, and the floor is covered with straw. For my work I receive two ladles of soup, two cups of coffee and an extra slice of bread. I think I will also earn 150 francs this month. It's not much because everything is very expensive. Sometimes we cook vegetables, which are available in the canteen from time to time, for example, a kilo of pickled cabbage costs 750. I cook vegetables like spinach, but unfortunately there are no spices available. Mr. Wildstrom, for whom I sent 30 francs, has not yet sent me a thing. Send the money back to us, because we don't have any money left.

Manfred, how did you come to the idea of America? We have no hopes, either for you or for ourselves. Nevertheless, we won't prevent you [from going], if that's your fate, because you asked us if we agree that you go on your own. I am enclosing a permit to this effect.

A few weeks ago Yakob Seligman died here, and in Gurs Sigmund Kirchheimer died of weakness. When I [...].

Best wishes for your birthday and congratulations on your bar mitzvah.[51] I wish you everything that a mother can wish for her son. Good luck in Toulouse, also from Father who is not here at the moment. Aunt Elsa writes that she hasn't heard from you for some time.

> That's all for today. Kisses from the
> bottom of my heart, from your Mother

Fred: My bar mitzvah was held in a cellar. We were living the normal life of boys of our age. I don't remember whether religion played an important role in our everyday lives, but like any boy approaching the age of thirteen, I wanted to celebrate my bar mitzvah. At the time I was influenced by one of my good friends, Karl (Uri) Landau. I joined him for morning prayers. I am convinced that Karl was deeply religious, but I'm not so sure about the strength of my own faith. Nevertheless I wanted to mark my bar mitzvah in some way, both because I felt it was the right thing to do, and because I knew it would greatly please my parents. The nearest Jewish community to Aspet was Toulouse. The necessary arrangements were made and I was taken to Toulouse. There, in a cellar, hidden from the eyes of strangers and the police above, I read a section of the Torah portion of the week. The event occurred in February 1942. The

---

51　Manfred went up to the Torah in the Toulouse synagogue. The ceremony was arranged by the Jewish underground. They prepared the bar mitzvah and brought Rabbi Paul Roitman, an underground activist, to conduct it.

ceremony was not attended by anyone I knew – neither friends nor family – although at one point Mother hoped she would be able to come. All those present were members of the Toulouse community, who saw in my bar mitzvah a declaration of faith and reaffirmation of life in spite of the fact that deportations from France were in progress.

Menachem: In the 1970s, I met Rabbi Roitman in a Jerusalem synagogue, and he told me about the ceremony he had arranged for Manfred. While Rabbi Roitman was telling the story, he didn't know the identity of the boy who went up to the Torah, or what became of him; and he certainly had no idea I was his brother.

Fred: I received a small picture as a gift, but I lost it. As I read the letters today, I can better comprehend the significance of my bar mitzvah for my parents, and how this particular event emphasized the disruption of the ties linking them with their children.

[21]

Rivesaltes, [...] February 1942
Dear Manfred and Heinz, we were very pleased with your letter. We can see you are well, we are also well, thank God. Best wishes for your birthday and bar mitzvah. Today your letter arrived (of January 26th) and we were happy to read that you are healthy and to learn about your school reports. I see, Heinz, that you enjoy school. Can you send us anything? I'm working in the stables again. Apart from that there's no news. We hope to hear from you soon. Tell us about the [...].

All the best and kisses, from your Father

My dear children,

I hope you received my letter. Mr. [...] sent me a reply, it seems that I will be given a permit. Mr. [Bloch] sent you a telegram on

Monday with an answer form. Did you get it? The rabbi says that your bar mitzvah is this week. How time flies, you're a big boy already. Have you heard anything about America? I'm pleased with my new work. I'm anxious to know if I'll get a permit to go to Toulouse, perhaps I'll get one because I'm working. I have a work certificate. What's news with you? It's very cold here and stormy all day.

The telegram came today, Wednesday. Congratulations from the bottom of my heart. It's not certain that I will be able to come.

Hoping to see you soon, I kiss you with all my heart.

Your Mother who loves you

[22]

Gurs, 2nd March 1942
Dear Manfred and Heinz,

We were happy to receive your letter of January 18th and to know you are well. We often hear from Inge. She is in a good place and well looked after. As far as we know your parents are well. I am sorry to give you the sad news that your grandmother has died. It came as a surprise to us all. At least she is spared further suffering.[52]

Manfred, I see you received lovely presents. With God's help we will make it up to you when we return home. I'm pleased the cold and rainy winter has passed. I don't know what else to write to you.

Heartfelt wishes from your Uncle Moritz

---

52 Grandmother Mina died in Gurs on February 26, 1942, at the age of seventy-two.

[23]

Gurs, 12th March 1942
Dear Manfred and Heinz,

I received your lovely letter, Manfred, thank you. To my great
regret Grandmother never got to read it. Imagine, Grandmother
isn't with us any more. The last few weeks have been very hard
for me, that's why I didn't write to you, my dear children. Imagine
how happy we would have been to celebrate your bar mitzvah
together with your parents. I wish you, belatedly, everything you
wish yourself, especially health. Be good, so we can take pleasure
in you and you will be a support to your parents. Write soon,
even though I'm not in the mood for writing letters, as you can
imagine. Now I am alone here. Tell Heinz he should write as well.

All the best and kisses, from your Uncle Emanuel

We have moved from block E to block F. Note the new address.
When I have the opportunity I will send you the bar mitzvah
present. I hope we will meet.

[24]

Rivesaltes, 19th May, 1942
My dear children,

I hope you are well, we are too. I was very surprised to receive a
parcel from you today. It made us very happy and all the things will
come in very useful. There were two small boxes of cheese, one was
open and nearly empty, some peas […], 5 hardboiled eggs. It would
have been better to send them raw. My neighbor in the next bed,
Mrs. Levy, often receives parcels. She's the "princess" of the Levy
family, who worked with Father in the kitchen in Gurs. Next to her
is Mrs. Kayem, Irene's mother, and next to her – Irma Heumann.

These three women receive lots of parcels every week, but they never share with each other. What can I say, they're lucky! On my other side is Mrs. Kahn with Irene from barrack 20 in Gurs. We have a dining barrack, with Spanish workers. Four times a week – Sundays, Tuesday, Wednesday and Thursdays – we get a little meat, a ladle of soup, a slice of bread, sometimes some cheese and wine. Lately we've sometimes had a little chocolate or cherries from the Secours Suisse.[53] In the morning I get two boxes of pea-flour soup because I only weigh 43 kilograms. Father gets one box, because he still weighs 51 kilograms. That's how we keep going somehow… The two white horses that Father works with are very wild, and I'm afraid something will happen to him. We received a letter from Aunt Elsa. The Quakers brought us a few hundred francs yesterday. Ask Mr. Wildstrom if he would be willing to send me a parcel, naturally I will send him money. Send uncooked eggs, so I can make an "Einlauf" soup or something else. I wrote twice to Ludwig at Les Milles[54] but he doesn't reply. Mr. Levy from Toulouse doesn't reply either. I'll write again. Once I sent him 50 francs.

What is Heinz doing? I'm pleased he enjoys school. Father isn't here at the moment, and I want to send off the letter.

All the best and kisses, from your Mother who loves you

[25]

Rivesaltes, 5th June 1942
My dearest children,

I received your letter on Monday and I see you are healthy, thank God, that's the main thing. Miss Salomon was here.

She said the Aspet children will come to us on July 15th. A horse bit Father on his arm. He has been hospitalized in Perpignan. Thank God his condition is improving. He has been there for

---

53 One of the welfare organizations with access to the camp.
54 Another camp. We don't remember the people referred to.

14 days. I was allowed to visit him last week, he doesn't need to lie down any more. The things that can happen to a person! Manfred, what do you mean when you say I'm not satisfied? When did I complain to you? Ruth Kallman[55] came to visit her parents. She was here for one day. Her father is also in hospital in Perpignan, but in a different hospital. Father is in the surgical ward.

What is Leo Rosenberg doing? His father is the head storekeeper here. He has his own room and he's already prepared an extra bed in preparation for Leo's arrival. Leo looks fat in the photograph. We can't see you clearly, you're standing in the back. Ruth Kallman looks wonderful. I am enclosing a few stamps. I have been hearing again about children traveling to Marseilles for the journey to America – I would like to see that you also have such good fortune. Ruth Pulm, who was with the Kohn family in Sinsheim, left on the earlier transport. Her mother and deaf Irma Kohn went to see her off in Marseilles. Ludwig Kaufmann[56] doesn't reply to my letters anymore. I received a new siddur [prayer book] from Mr. Bloch. I'll send it to you when I have money for postage. I didn't get a tallit [prayer shawl] or tefillin [phylacteries]. Write to Mr. Levy in Toulouse, I haven't heard from him. It's very hot here.

Kisses, Mother

Perpignan, 21st June 1942
Dear Manfred and Heinz,

I received your letter and I see you are healthy and happy. I was pleased to read that you know French well – I'm breaking my teeth on it.[57] Even Mother knows a little French. I'm doing well, staying in the hospital a few more days because the wound in my

---

55 One of the Aspet children.

56 A relative of ours who lived in America.

57 In the original: "da steht mir ein Ochs am Berg" which translates as "It stands like an ox on a hill," meaning, "like a stubborn ox unwilling to move and climb the hill."

arm hasn't entirely healed. Mr. Kallmann[58] is in the next bed. He is unable to walk. I write his letters for him – don't tell his son about his condition.

You want to know what I do all day? I run around all day and sleep so I won't think of the hunger. Now we must eat all the bread we never wanted to eat, the food you never wanted to eat and brought home from school in Heidelberg. Sometimes I argued with Mother over food, and I wasn't always right. I also argued with her about *Wicked Oli*.[59] I haven't heard anything from them, neither do I wish to know anything at all about the relatives. Aunt Alma is the same, she who has so many relatives. Don't write to Uncle Moritz about what I said. We can only rely on ourselves, we should only remain healthy until these troubles pass and we emerge from the vale of tears. Mother came to visit me. She has a slender figure. Think about it, it's nearly two years since we left home, far from the good food. It's never possible to eat until you're full. The same goes for everything.

I don't have any stamps. If I get some, I'll send them to you. Be good children and study. I hope I will yet merit to see good times with you both and with Mother. For a long time I thought that something would happen to Grandmother. Perhaps it's better now, she's at rest. It was so nice when we came to visit her in Neidenstein. Do you have news from Emanuel?

Write soon, all the best and kisses, from your Father

[27]

23rd June 1942
To: Elsa Mayer, Clifton Gardens, London, England
From: Manfred Mayer, Children's Home, Aspet, France

---

58 The father of Max and Ruth, who were with us in Aspet.
59 The emphasis is in the original text. We don't remember who Oli was – possibly one of our relatives who emigrated overseas, promised to help, but didn't stand by his word.

We are well, so is Mother. Father is in hospital, bitten by a horse. His condition is improving. Hoping you are well. Our parents are still in camp.

Kisses, Manfred

Reply
Many thanks. I am well. News from Helmut, he is well. Regards to you all. I don't hear from you. Mother wrote to me about Father. I wish him a complete recovery.

Kisses, Elsa[60]

[28]

Rivesaltes, 9th July 1942
My most precious children,

I received your letter and see you are well. Heinz, I am most surprised that you don't listen to Manfred, after all you are a big boy and sensible as well! Miss Salomon came. She is finding out whether you can come to visit during the vacation. Don't get your hopes up too soon. Mr. Rosenberg is preparing a room with beds for you.

Yesterday Father came back unexpectedly, thank God. He has completely recovered. Today he went back to work. On Saturday approximately 200 people arrived from Gurs. Some of them are in my barrack. Among them are Betty Yakob of the Wurtzweiler family. Mr. Yakob also works in the stables. One lady told me that Emanuel came to her barrack every day to visit a Miss Bodenheimer from Bretten. Emanuel lights the kitchen stoves for the extras, he feels well. I'll tell you everything when you come. Some people also came from Recebedou.[61] Aunt Berta works in the kitchen there.

---

60 Communication by telegram with Aunt Elsa. Telegrams were sent through the Red Cross.
61 One of the camps in southern France.

Everyone likes her. More people are expected from Gurs. Various people with relatives in France have been released. I would go to work, but for the time being I'm staying with Father. Write soon. We just this minute received tomato soup. I would like to send you some fruit, but I'll wait until you come. In the canteen you can get peaches, apricots and pears. Don't you have any fruit? We have no potatoes. Four times a week we get a little meat. In the morning I get a supplement of two ladles of peas porridge with vitamins and a spoonful of Germalse – a kind of flour intended for children. We have straw sacks. In block J there are beds. We eat in the dining room. There are tables and benches there. The floor is full of stones – you'll see everything when you come.

>   Kisses from your Mother who loves you.
>   Please, don't fight with each other.

My dear Manfred and Heinz, I understand you received my letter of 9th June. As you can see, I returned to Mother, and I've gone back to work.

Heinz, Manfred complained that you don't listen to him. You must pay attention to him – he's older than you! It's very hot here. I am pleased to be out of hospital, because the boredom was driving me mad. Kallmann is a little better. Write soon.

>   All the best and kisses from your Father

[29]

Rivesaltes, 10th August 1942[62]
My dear children,

I want to write a few lines quickly before the journey. Seeing that we are leaving and we are only permitted to take one piece of hand luggage, I sent you the chest of clothes yesterday evening.

---

62 This is the final letter from our parents.

If you go to America, take with you whatever is necessary. With the help of God, perhaps we will also get there. Give our regards to Aunt Elsa when you write to her. I don't know whether we'll be able to write to you – perhaps through the Red Cross. Be good children.

Your Mother, who loves you

My dear children,
Just a few lines before we leave – I don't know where we're going. We don't in the least regret leaving you behind, you are safer where you are. Perhaps you'll hear everything.

Be well. All the best and kisses from your Mother.[63]

Dear Manfred and Heinz, be good to one another – that's my greatest concern.

[30]

London, 15th September 1942
My darling children Manfred and Heinz,

On Rosh Hashanah[64] I received your letter of 20th August. I am pleased to know you are well. I am too. I am waiting for a letter from Helmut. It's terrible not to hear anything for so long. I don't hear very often from Uncle Moritz either. I hope they are still in the same place. I always attach a reply form to my letter, this time I'm attaching two. I don't know if the regulations permit me to send a photograph of myself, I'll try to find out. I received your photos. I already wrote to you about them.

Dear children, have you heard anything from your parents? Let me know. May God help them. Trust in Him, the All Powerful,

---

63 Father was apparently very agitated, signing the letter "your Mother" instead of "your Father."
64 September 12-13, 1942.

who has never abandoned us and will not abandon us now. That is my hope and my prayer. Be strong, my children, and make sure you stay healthy. I will not abandon you. Now I am your aunt, and I will remain so in the future as well, as much as I am able.

My English is so-so, and I continue to learn. I already wrote to tell you where I work. I gave your address to a lady, so perhaps some day you'll receive a parcel, but don't get your hopes up. Despite everything I am happy to see that there are still some people who have a heart. May God help us and may we meet again soon. Then I'll tell you everything. We must hope for the best and trust in God. Remain healthy together. I am pleased to hear that Uncle Moritz and Uncle Emanuel are still there and they're still working – that helps a lot.

I see that you, Heinz, also know how to write nice letters. Manfred, I'm collecting as many stamps as I can. Where is Seppel?[65] I'm curious to know where the girl is from!

I'll end here. God bless you and kisses from your aunt who loves you, Aunt Elsa. Be well, dear children.

---

65 One of our relatives, who lived with us at 10 Kirchestrasse and came with us to Gurs.

We Are Alone

It is difficult for us to describe this stage of our lives, because it was terrible. It reopens wounds that never quite healed and the pain burns as keenly as ever, despite the intervening years. Nevertheless, we feel we have no choice but to talk about it for our sake and for those who follow us.

Fred: In the early summer of 1942, some fifteen months after parting from our parents, we were informed that we could visit them in the camp. We were very excited and began preparing for our visit. We hoarded food, especially bread, which we hid in shoe boxes under the mattresses to bring to our parents.

Menachem: Uri Landau, one of the leaders of the Aspet group of forty-eight, asked Mr. Wildstrom (a Jew hiding in the village) whether it was permissible to steal food for our parents who were starving in the camp. After considering the question from all angles he sagely decreed that it was not a sin. It's interesting to note that the older children were preoccupied with the moral aspects. The religious-ethical implications didn't bother me a bit.

As it turned out, the visit never took place. Our guardian angel, Andrée Salomon of OSE, prevented it. She convinced the parents not to see their children in order not to place them in danger. Unknown to us kids, there was a dark sense of foreboding among the adults – terrible and unbelievable rumors of indescribable happenings in the East, in Poland. By this time, in mid-1942, the Auschwitz monster was fully alive and voracious. It had already devoured three million in the East. Now the Nazis turned west to force the Jews of Belgium, Holland, Germany, Norway, and France into its ravenous jaws. In the 1980s, a short time before she died, Andrée told me the only reason she dared demand such a sacrifice of our parents was because she had been reliably informed that anyone entering the camp would not be permitted to leave. In fact, some parents were unable to pass up the chance of seeing their children once more and their children were sent with them to Auschwitz. This was what happened to Gunther Hausmann, one of our group of forty eight. His death in Auschwitz is documented.

Fred: How in Heaven did we escape this fate and why? Did our parents have a premonition of what awaited them? Was it because of the care taken by others to hide us? Was it luck? For the past fifty years these questions have haunted us. Even our momentous, unforgettable trip together to Auschwitz in 1990, walking their "final walk" – from the train disembarkation ramp to the gas chamber – didn't provide answers or give us peace of mind.

I have often asked myself why our parents never escaped from Gurs or Rivesaltes. Technically, it was entirely possible. What do you think, Menachem?

Menachem: There is no simple answer. First of all, they didn't know what awaited them: who could have imagined it? They must have been convinced things couldn't get any worse. The Germans used clever subterfuges to make them believe they would be relocated to better conditions where work was available. Remember these were people in their prime of life, in their forties. Furthermore, they were educated in Germany, where obedience to orders was axiomatic. Also, they probably didn't believe they could save themselves. Even if they had succeeded in getting out of the camp without permission, they had no citizenship, no ID, no means of survival, no knowledge of French, and they looked like prisoners. Perhaps they also took comfort in the knowledge that we were sheltered, and they didn't want to take us out of Aspet. From their point of view, it would make no sense to escape without us, because then all contact with us would be lost.

That entire spring of 1942, trainloads of deportees were conveyed eastward at a steadily increasing rate. Certainly we kids at Aspet had no inkling of what was happening. The big question remains: how much did the others know? Today we are aware that the chimneys of Auschwitz never stopped belching smoke. The killing machine was operating at full steam...

After the Wannsee Conference on January 21, 1942, Adolf Eichmann instructed Dannecker, his deputy in France, to deport 10,000 Jews to the East. The first train set out at the end of March, 1942, followed by others, one after the other. All this was taking place while we, in our innocence, were hoarding bread for our parents.

In May, Heydrich – Eichmann's commanding officer – arrived in Paris to finalize with the Vichy chief of police the deportation of "stateless" Jews – those without nationality. Obviously, this category included those German-born Jews whose citizenship had been revoked by the Germans, including us. The German demands coincided perfectly with the desire of the French to be rid of the Jews. The French cooperated willingly, and in fact did most of the work for the Germans, expediting the process of deportation by using their own police and railways. Vichy France was the only European country apart from Bulgaria to hand Jews from areas not directly under the control of the German military over to the Nazis.

Fred: On August 10, 1942, our parents sent their last letter. Did they have any inkling of what was in store for them? The contents and tone of their letter indicate that they were nervous and apprehensive. In his panic and confusion, Father even signed "Kisses from your Mother" instead of "your Father." We think they believed they were being resettled somewhere in Eastern Europe, as the Germans informed them. We hope they didn't know what lay ahead at the end of the line – Auschwitz.

Menachem: Today we know they were taken from Rivesaltes to Drancy transit camp, some five kilometers outside of Paris. Four days later, on August 14, they set off on their final journey. We unearthed this information in November 1998 at the Centre de Documentation Juive in Paris, where we also found the German SS dispatch orders for the transport that brought them to Auschwitz.

The Security Services
Paris, 14th August 1942
Urgent, Immediate, Top Secret
To: National Security Headquarters, Section IVB4
SS Colonel Eichmann, A.I.V.O. – Berlin
To: Oranienburg Concentration Camp Headquarters
To: Auschwitz Concentration Camp
On 14th August 1942 at 8:55 freight train no. D901/ 19 left Le Bourget-Drancy station for Auschwitz with a total of 1,000 Jews (including, for the first time, children). All those involved received appropriate instructions.
The commanding officer of the transport is Sergeant-Major Krupp. He has been provided with a duplicate list of all those in the transport.
As always, means for 14 days have been provided for each Jew.
On orders,
(-) Roethke
Obersturmführer

Father was forty-eight and Mother was forty-four. It is nearly certain that they were killed upon arrival at Auschwitz.

Four days earlier, transport no. 17 (train 911/12) rolled eastward bearing Uncle Moritz (forty-four years old) and Aunt Alma (thirty-one), Ingrid's parents. Transport no. 12, two days previously, carried Uncle Emanuel (thirty-nine years old). Grandmother Mina died in Gurs.

The whole immediate family perished; not by natural disaster, but by the inhuman hand of man. We were on our own.

Fred: That train number 19 on August 14, 1942. On the basis of what we know today I have tried countless times to imagine our parents' anguish and distress on that endless journey into the unknown…the locomotive pulling those cattle cars… the train crossing France, Germany, Austria, Czechoslovakia, finally reaching Poland. Many stops… the train is frequently shunted to a siding, to permit troop transports to move up the line on their way to and from the Russian front. (This at the height of the war with Russia – the Germans devote their manpower, transport, and enthusiasm to their priority – killing the Jews.)

I see them crowded together, unable to move, with no food, water, or sanitary conditions – men, women and children. Day followed night; night, day… For three to four days. What were they thinking? What was on their minds? What agony.

To this day whenever a train passes, whenever I hear the shriek of a train's whistle and the clacking sound of wheels rolling over railroad track, that same picture appears before me. I try to push it away, but it always returns. Perhaps it's guilt for not sharing their fate.

We weren't there, but a young man named Albert Hollander was deported to Auschwitz two weeks later, on August 28. He survived. After the war he wrote: "We were crammed into cattle cars, unable to sit or move. We were wedged together, crushing one another. It was hell. During the day the temperature soared and the smell was unbearable. We arrived several days later, dehydrated and exhausted. Many were ill."[66] As we know, many people died on the trains during their frightful journey.

Another description of our parents' journey to Auschwitz can be found in the book written by Serge and Beate Klarsfeld, who published invaluable facts on the deportation of Jews from France. The book contains details of each deportation, including the names, origins, and birthdates of all 80,000 deportees. This excerpt is taken from Serge Klarsfeld's documentation of train #19:

The train contained 1,015 people, slightly more men than women. Most of the men were between the ages of 43-64… The women were

---

66 Quoted in Martin Gilbert, *The Holocaust*, New York 1985, p. 437.

between the ages of 39–64. There were more than 100 children. Upon their arrival in Auschwitz 115 of them passed the selection, all of them males aged 18-42. The other deportees were taken immediately to the gas chambers... Not a single woman or child was sent into the camp... To the best of our knowledge, when the war ended in 1945, only one person from this transport was still living. [Note: Selection here means picked for slave labor and spared the gas chamber for awhile. Those selected were tattooed with a number on the forearm; those going into the gas chamber were not.][67]

Menachem: Another testimony is provided by Professor Robert Weitz.[68] He describes the arrival of the train in the camp:

The people make their way along the platform. Two SS men stand in the center of the platform – one of them is a medical officer. The people pass before him. He indicates with his thumb or a stick whether they should go left or right. In this way two lines are formed. The line on the left is made up of people aged 20–45. The age group is flexible, depending on work requirements and the need for a work force – sometimes it includes people aged 16–55. Several young women are included in this line. The line on the right is made up of older men, elderly people, most of the women, children and those who are ill. The line on the left is led into the camp, from where they will be taken out on forced labor details. The line on the right goes to the crematorium. The people are unaware of this. The interpreter on duty informs them they are going to be showered and disinfected. They are taken into the "changing room." There are hooks on the walls to hang their clothes. They are asked to remember the number of their hook for when they emerge from the shower(!). The deception continues with the distribution of slivers of soap. The ruse is successful.

67 Serge Klarsfeld, *Le Mémorial de la Déportation des Juifs de France*, Paris 1978.

68 Poliakov, *Harvest of Hate*, p. 203.

Shower heads protrude from the ceiling of the "shower room..."
Zyklon B poison gas pellets are inserted through apertures in the
ceiling. The screaming can be heard for three to ten minutes.

Fred: We forego the details of the horror that followed. We
felt the need to touch lightly on the inconceivable because of
what the two people we knew and loved experienced. All of us
can relate to two; but hundreds, thousands, yes, even millions?
Industrialized, technological, systematic murder in the twentieth
century, perpetrated by that most civilized nation – Germany?
It's inconceivable, but it happened! Yet despite the chilling facts,
testimonies from witnesses and numerous documents, some people
today question or even deny that the Holocaust ever happened.

This was the agony, the unspeakable torment and torture our
parents suffered. Two people from among millions...

Why? Many have asked this question, hundreds of books have
been written to explain the inexplicable... We believe it is because
of man's inhumanity to man. For years, the Germans wanted
nothing more than to get rid of the Jews but the countries of the
world refused to respond. New legislation in 1941 in the United
States slowed the rate of immigration to near zero. In October,
only a few dozen visas were granted daily. Switzerland closed its
borders. The British refused to accept any more refugees on the
grounds that it would inflame antisemitism in England. They had
also closed the gates of Palestine in deference to the Arabs. Spain
and Portugal were increasingly refusing to issue transit visas.

We are not surprised by the Nazis' behavior. We had ten years
of warnings and deeds... From the French however, we could
have expected more than handing over the Jews with impunity.
They could have said "No" without serious consequences, as
others did.

The Allies (the United States and Britain) knew what was
happening as early as 1942, but stopping this slaughter never
became an issue. For example, they over flew Auschwitz frequently
and could have bombed the installations and rail lines to slow the
process. The Vatican remained silent in spite of the overwhelming

facts at its disposal. Not once during the war did the Pope use the word Jew or Nazi to protest the killings.

As early as 1938, the nations of the world turned their collective backs on the pleas for immigration expressed at the Evian Conference. Out of the thirty-two countries represented, only the little island of the Dominican Republic offered to take in five hundred people. Hitler could rightly boast that nobody wanted the Jews.

Yes, the deed was done by the Germans and their helpers, but it was the world's apathy if not antipathy that made it possible.

The Danes and the Italians

We want to close this darkest of chapters with a word about Denmark and Italy. In October 1943, while occupied by the Germans, the Danes were able to rescue the majority of the Jews in their country. We wish to emphasize this act as a demonstration of what could be done by a government and people with basic human decency – in stark contrast to Vichy France. Surprisingly, a German official warned the Danish authorities about the imminent deportation of the Jews. The Danes got word to the Jews, hid them, and eventually ferried over 7,000 of them across the North Sea at night in small fishing boats to neutral Sweden.

Mussolini, in spite of the fact that he was Hitler's ally, steadfastly refused to hand over Italy's Jews in the face of repeated German demands. Only after Mussolini was deposed and the Germans occupied the country, did the Jews become vulnerable to deportation.

What does all this mean to us, what lessons should we draw?

Listen to the pleas of your fellow man; don't turn your back. Stamp out the hatemongers before they do too much damage. Show no tolerance toward those who would divide humanity into better and lesser. Fight the deniers.

We are convinced of this wisdom: "Those who ignore history are bound to relive it."

Our Last Stop Together: Toulouse

Menachem: All contact with our parents had been lost. We had no idea where they were or what had happened to them.

Following the Allied invasion of North Africa and the swift capitulation of the Vichy forces on November 11, 1942, Germany occupied southern France, which had been under Vichy control. The immediate result of the occupation was that the Jews in this region of France were subjected to relentless persecution.

The local French authorities and the Germans were well aware of our presence in Aspet. Andrée Salomon of OSE decided, for obvious reasons, to disperse us in various hiding places. The forty-eight of us and another 5,000 or so children in various orphanages were like sitting ducks, ready to be picked up in one raid by the Germans. On February 21, 1943, the Quakers transported several children, including Manfred and myself, to the Chateau de Larade orphanage in Toulouse.

I remember hearing a burst of automatic fire as we descended from the train in Toulouse. We hid in the yard of a nearby house until the danger was past.

The orphanage was in a chateau surrounded by fields and trees and owned by the Catholic Church. It had been turned into a refuge for children fleeing to France to escape the 1936–1939 Civil War in neighboring Spain. On our arrival we were greeted by the director of the orphanage, Señor Galy, a Spaniard.

The following morning, we began to attend the local school, named for Jules Ferry. I enjoyed going to school and I also liked studying. The school day was long, from morning to evening, with a lunch break at the chateau, so we covered the distance between the school and the chateau four times each day. When we left in the morning we wore a uniform – a long gray tunic which also served to protect our clothes. I remember that my teacher in Toulouse was Monsieur Raymond Guilhelm, or – as we called him – "Père Guillaume." I was eleven years old and in the sixth grade.

Fred: About a month after arriving in Toulouse, I was separated from my brother, because it was decided to move all children above the age of fourteen to a different place – a home for teenagers operated by the Eclaireurs Israelites de France (EIF), the French-Jewish Boy Scouts, in the town of Moissac in the Tam-et-Garonne. We didn't meet again for three and a half years, when I went to visit him in Switzerland after the war.[69]

Menachem: I don't remember the actual parting, or what they told us. There are many important things that I don't remember...

In 1985, I visited Jacqueline Sallebert, who took care of us in Aspet. She opened a drawer, took out a letter and said: "Here's the letter you sent me a week after your arrival in Toulouse. I don't know why I kept it all these years." I was astonished – I hardly remembered Jacqueline, and I certainly didn't remember writing to her. I asked whether she remembered why I wrote to her. She replied: "I was a kind of mother figure for you. You were very attached to me, you came to me to be petted. I was very fond of you, you were my 'chouchou' (sweetie)." The letter describes life in the orphanage and lessons in the classroom. It includes the following:

> The teacher showed my exercise book and that of another student
> to the whole class. In the other boy's book were only "eggs"[70]
> and mine had only tens... The teacher shouted, he said: "These

---

69 This was the parting of our ways. Menachem continues his story
    until our next meeting, in autumn 1946.
70 Zeros.

Germans are teaching you French!"[71] Each day he says to me:
"You try hard, you are the best!"

With such encouragement it's no wonder I enjoyed school.

In 1998, I visited Toulouse, seeking the school that held such
bittersweet memories. Fifty-four years later, I discovered several
documents from that period in the school archives. Next to my
name is written: "Gifted and disciplined" – it seems that my self-
image, as expressed in my letter to Jacqueline, was accurate. The
comment on my brother reads: "Very diligent, very disciplined.
Good student."

I've forgotten most of the pranks – and the punishments
they earned me – but I haven't forgotten the praise and positive
support I received from time to time. I think they influenced my
conduct and the molding of my character in the long run far more
than the punishments. This may lead to a general conclusion –
we don't give enough positive reinforcement, as compared to
negative reinforcement.

I was constantly hungry in the chateau. I stole bread and other
things, and once I got caught, together with my good friend,
Alfred Stein. We had broken into the orphanage breadbox and
were busily filling our pockets with loot. One of our minders
took us by surprise. He asked why we were taking bread. Falsely
innocent we replied: "Us? Taking bread?" but he wasn't fooled.
He looked at our bulging pockets and went away without a
word. That was proof, if any were needed, that silence can speak
more loudly and to better effect than a thousand words or even
a sound beating. From that day, I never touched anything that
did not belong to me.

Despite the hunger, we tried to eat kosher food. Whenever
we suspected that the meat in a cooked dish was ham or bacon,
we removed it before eating. Sometimes they served us lobster,
which I adored – we never ate lobster in Hoffenheim, so I had

---

71 In the eyes of the local people, we were the Germans whom they
    detested.

no idea whether it was kosher or not. It was fascinating to see how they cooked the lobsters, throwing them into boiling water until they turned red.

I made friends with the Spanish gardener, whose name I forget. He was a Republican soldier, on the losing side in the Spanish Civil War. He told me many war stories, proudly describing Andalusia, which was where he hailed from.

At the orphanage they taught me how to conceal my identity, which wasn't easy with my German accent. They showed me ways to escape from the chateau, in case the Gestapo or the French militia ever took us by surprise. They also changed my name to Henri. Yet despite these precautions, I wasn't always careful. One day while playing in the public park, a speck of dust flew into my eye. A German soldier of the Wehrmacht who was sitting on a bench called me over, sat me on his knee, and removed the speck while chatting with me in German... From the look on his face, which has remained with me to this day, I am convinced he knew who I was (or rather, what I was)... Apparently they weren't all Nazis.

As the date of the Allied invasion drew nearer, the bombardments became heavier and more frequent. The sky was filled with hundreds of B-29 bombers.

On May 4, 1944, I was shaken awake in the early morning and told that we must leave.

PART II

Separate
Ways

Menachem: Wandering in Switzerland

Escape from France to Switzerland

While the Allies were making final preparations to invade the Continent (on June 6, 1944), the Vichy police in Toulouse learned that Jewish children were hiding in the Chateau de Larade. When OSE got wind of this, Andrée Salomon – a key activist in the organization – decided there was no time to lose; we must be smuggled into Switzerland without delay.

At the beginning of May, we traveled under assumed names to the French Alps, ostensibly for some rest and recreation. Our group consisted of fifteen children accompanied by several women, members of OSE, operating through the Jewish underground known as "La Sixième" (The Sixth).[72] Unfortunately, I don't remember their names. Neither do I remember much about the journey itself. I only remember Lyons, our first stop, where we spent the night in an enormous room surrounded by huge mirrors and heavy red drapes.

Many years later, Andrée Salomon filled in the gaps when we met in Jerusalem in the 1980s. She told me that after one abortive attempt to cross the border, we traveled by train to the village of Annemasse, a French-Swiss border town. Alighting at a nearby station, we continued our journey on foot. Our guides were fully aware that Gestapo and border guards lay in wait everywhere. They risked their lives for us.

---

72 Fred will discuss this in more detail later on.

I remember hurrying through a dark forest with our guides and the border smuggler. Suddenly he said: "Here's the border. On the other side of the fence is Switzerland." We were instructed to crawl under the wire. I did what I was told, and when I stood up – a soldier was standing before me. I was in shock! He was dressed in a green uniform, and I was sure he was a German soldier. It's a pity nobody bothered to tell me that the Swiss border guards also wore green uniforms! The border guards escorted us to a kind of reception and screening center in Geneva, the Camp de Triage Claparède.

And so I was snatched from the talons of the Nazis. It happened in the afternoon of Thursday, May 25, 1944.

When we arrived at the screening center I was interrogated by the Swiss border police. Our rescuers had prepared us for this. Before arriving at the Swiss border they warned us not to divulge any information, including the names of our guides or the smuggler. We were told to start crying if they pressed us too much. I don't remember exactly what they asked us, but I assume that by the end of May 1944 the Swiss authorities had a pretty clear idea of which way the war was going. At any rate, they weren't very aggressive.

In 1994, I was informed that the archives of the Swiss Federal Police contained personal files on all refugees during the war years. Apparently the Swiss authorities kept close watch on each refugee, including the children. After submitting numerous requests, I received a copy of my personal record – File No. 22838 – which provided many details that I had either forgotten or suppressed.

The file includes the following: "Incursion [into Switzerland] occurred near Seral 2 border station on May 25, 1944, at approximately 13:00." In my statement, I am quoted as saying: "I am part of a group of children that was organized in Lyons. The ladies accompanied us, and the border smugglers showed us the way... No, I don't know their names... Yes, we crossed the border in secret..."

Switzerland is situated in the heart of Europe. It borders on Germany, Austria, Italy, and France. Despite its geographic location, or perhaps because of it, Switzerland has not been at war for many years. During the Second World War, it maintained neutrality, was not directly involved in any power struggles, and committed no atrocities, but its neutrality stemmed from convenience rather than morality.

Switzerland was reputed to be a safe haven for refugees, but in fact, it was only the Swiss banks that opened their doors to Jewish money; the gates did not part willingly for Jewish refugees. Swiss authorities barred the entry of many Jews seeking asylum in their country and to make quite sure they could easily spot them, as early as 1938 they insisted that the Nazis stamp the letter J (Jude) on the passports of German and Austrian Jews. With hindsight, it is clear that this demand facilitated the Nazis' plan to exterminate the Jews. Moreover, in August 1942, when the Nazi killing machine had swung into high gear, Switzerland passed a law that in effect hermetically sealed her borders. The law decreed that Jews were refugees for racial rather than political reasons(!) and must therefore be banished to Germany or France. In other words, they were to be handed over to their persecutors. It was only due to public pressure that in September 1942, the Swiss police agreed to admit children up to the age of sixteen (apparently this is what saved me), and a few exceptional cases. Everyone else was turned over to the Gestapo. The exact figure of those refused entry into Switzerland is not known, but it is generally assumed to be more than 30,000.

Personally, I can't complain – I was one of the 22,000 Jews who found asylum in Switzerland.

In the morning of June 6, fourteen days after I arrived, the Allies landed in France, opening the second front in the west. The war continued for another eleven months, ending on May 8, 1945, but the end of the war did not signal the end of my wanderings. I did not leave until 1948, when I made my way to Israel. I spent more than four years in Switzerland. During that time I drifted from place to place the length and breadth of the country. I was sent to nine separate institutions; in some of them I spent no more than a few days, in others – months and even a year or more.

As I mentioned at the beginning, I have either forgotten or suppressed a great deal. The sequence of events and places here recorded is based on scraps of memory, statements, documents, and certificates.

First stop: Geneva, Claparede Screening Center

I arrived at Claparede Screening Center in Geneva, where I was subjected to medical and psychological tests. I was twelve years old.

Among other things, they asked if I want to be in a religious framework. For some reason I remember my reply, and the documents in my personal file attest to it. I replied: "I don't care." Looking back, it's quite clear that I didn't understand the question. I made no distinction between religious and secular. In my parents' house, as far as I can remember, our lifestyle was traditional and tolerant. In any event, my reply – or fate, perhaps – eventually resulted in my referral to the ultra-Orthodox faction of Agudas Israel Poalei Agudas Israel.

Second stop: Geneva, Camp Henri Dunant

On June 16, 1944, the Red Cross sent me to Camp Henri Dunant. I remember absolutely nothing about this place, relying only on documents. My personal file includes the following information:

Child's health: good, slightly too thin

No particular preference for religious placement. Wants to go to school.

Speaks German, French, and a little Spanish.

Very pleasant and engaging.

Here I was given a refugee identity card – Flüchtlingsausweis no. 24799.

Third stop: Schwandibach, Waldrosli

In the summer of 1944, July 27 to be exact, I traveled in a yellow mail bus over the mountains in the Bern canton. The bus stopped at a little village, Schwandibach, where I was placed in the Waldrosli children's home.

It was a typical Swiss village nestled in a sloping valley, in the heart of a green meadow, surrounded by fruit trees. I particularly remember a walnut tree. I was deeply impressed to learn I could collect all the nuts that dropped on the ground and eat them to my heart's content...

I arrived during the long vacation. I don't recall why I didn't go to school at the beginning of the school year. I remember the educator, Haim Gitler, who took me under his wing for some reason. On one occasion he discussed with me – a boy of twelve – whether I should be separated from Alfred, my good friend from the camp, because he was a bad influence on me. The fact that my opinion was sought, after years of being treated like an object, made a deep impression on me. I tend to believe Haim was honestly concerned for me. In any event, I decided not to break with Alfred.

Fourth stop: Grub, Friedberg

On January 17, 1945, in the middle of winter, we were moved to Friedberg, an institution in the village of Grub, not far from the town of Saint Gallen in northeastern Switzerland and close to the German border. The day we arrived, the entire countryside was blanketed with snow.

During our stay we saw hundreds of planes carrying their cargo of bombs in the direction of Germany. I cannot remember whether I was at all aware of the significance of what I was seeing.

In the meantime I had arrived at bar mitzvah age. I began learning the Hebrew alphabet, and was taught to chant the Maftir – the part of the Torah portion that I would read to mark the occasion. Having no recollection of either my father's Jewish name or my own, I was called to the Torah as "Haim ben Avraham." I assume that "Haim" was chosen because of its similarity to Heinz. "Son of Abraham" – aren't we all? Our real names had been sent to us in the letter from our parents in Gurs, but it would take another three years until I learned the names from my big brother Manfred.

Fifth stop: Engelberg, Central Hotel

Three months later, on April 23, 1945, I was again transferred to a new place – my fifth move in eleven months. The journey took many hours; the train wound its way among the mountains, reaching an elevation of 1,050 meters before it arrived at Engelberg station. I found myself in a quiet, scenic resort village surrounded by snow-capped mountains, lakes, forests, and meadows. During the war years there were, of course, no foreign tourists; some of the empty hotels were used to house refugees.

"Alijah Heim" was located in the Central Hotel. It was a boys-only Zionist Orthodox establishment that prepared us for our transfer to Palestine. A similar arrangement existed for girls in another hotel, the Alpina. Altogether we were approximately one hundred children.

I spent quite a long time in Engelberg – certainly longer than any of my other stops. Altogether I was there for about one and a half years. I try to remember details about the place and what I did there, but I can't! Everything is foggy. I know I didn't attend school. At the hotel we were taught basic religious studies – Hebrew reading and writing, Torah, Jewish laws and customs, and later on they taught us some Mishnah.[73] From time to time I bought a local newspaper. I misbehaved and played many pranks, sometimes by myself, at other times inspired by my good friend Alfred. We were caught in the act several times, but I always managed to talk my way out of it.

The war finally ended. We all expected our parents to return from "over there," but it didn't happen and I resigned myself

---

73 The Mishnah is the civil and religious law code compiled around
    200 C.E. that is the basis for the legal discussions of the Talmud.

to the fact that I was an orphan. In truth I'd already been in this situation for the past five years. I had no idea what had really happened. Six months later, some boys joined us who were survivors of Buchenwald concentration camp. They told us stories and showed us photographs of the crematoria. Those pictures remain engraved in my memory. I don't recall whether the adults in charge attempted to provide any kind of psychological or explanatory counseling. What could they have done, anyway? Like the rest of us, they were stunned and helpless in face of the catastrophe.

At the end of August 1945, less than four months after the end of the war, a letter arrived from the Swiss Federal Police:

> According to information received from the Allies, it appears that German and Austrian refugees, including those whose citizenship was revoked, will soon be able to return home. In order to negotiate with the authorities and make the necessary preparations for their return, you are requested to complete the attached questionnaires.[74]

I remember that I filled in the questionnaire as follows: "I intend to emigrate to Palestine (Eretz Israel). I am scheduled to depart on one of the next transports." I had no way of knowing that I would continue my wanderings in Europe for the next two years.

My brother Manfred, from whom I had been separated two years earlier in Toulouse, located me through OSE. Aunt Elsa, who fled to England before war broke out, located us with the assistance of the Joint – my brother in France and me in Switzerland.

In November 1998, I found our file (some 77 documents) in the OSE archives in Paris. The archives of the International Alliance Organization yielded another seven documents, including one from my brother granting permission for me to emigrate to Israel. From correspondence between my brother and Aunt Elsa and between the two of them and various organizations – OSE, the

---

74 Personal file no. 22838. Schweizerisches Bundesarchiv, Bern.

Joint, the Swiss Red Cross, SHEK,[75] the Swiss association to assist the children of refugees, and the Federal Police – one can learn a great deal about the many activities undertaken on behalf of the stateless refugees. The involvement of the Swiss authorities was mainly motivated by the fact that our presence was a burden to them and they wanted to be rid of us as soon as possible. In contrast, the welfare and rescue organizations were motivated by the best of intentions, but during that first period after the war they were so swamped with work that they were unable to pay attention to every little detail. This is the only excuse I can think of to explain why nobody tried to unite me with my brother so we could begin rebuilding our lives together.

The OSE file reveals that when France was liberated, while the war in Europe continued to rage, extensive correspondence was conducted about our future. We learn, for example, that in April there was already talk of us traveling to Palestine. It further transpires that in the fall of 1942, while we were still in Aspet together, we were granted entry permits to England. In connection with this, the file contains correspondence with Manfred on the question of whether, now the war was over, he would like to move to England together with me. Other letters deal with the possibility of my joining him in France. I was entirely unaware of this flourishing correspondence – certainly I had no idea that my sixteen-year-old brother had decided to complete his studies as an electrician before we made our way to Palestine. I was therefore faced with foregone conclusions.

In the second half of 1946, Manfred's plans changed, and he decided to emigrate to the United States. As he says, he was motivated by several factors. He wanted to sever all ties with the "old country"; he felt the need to flee from his past and from his destiny as a Jew. A new world beckoned from across the sea. In my opinion, his flight did not end when he crossed the ocean. I think his choice of career, as a space engineer, also represents a kind of flight, as far as possible, to outer space...

---

75 Schweizer Hilfswerk für Emigrantenkinder.

In the fall of that year, several months before his departure, Manfred came to visit me in Engelberg. He tried to persuade me to join him, but I refused, insisting that I wanted to go to Palestine. I was fourteen at the time, and very much influenced by my teachers and counselors, so I don't think this was an independent decision on my part. Sometimes I ask myself what right they had to separate two brothers, the only survivors of one whole family?

That's how my fate was decided. That's how my life came to take the path it did. Sometimes we control events and make choices, but most of the time it only seems that way, because our actions are dictated by circumstances over which we have no control. Life is a complicated system of give-and-take. The best thing to do is to adapt to situations which we cannot control and shape those we can.

Fred: Living in Hiding

Fred: On April 3, 1943, I was moved to the town of Moissac in southwest France, and taken to an institution run by the Jewish Scout Movement EIF.[76] My brother Heinz remained behind in Toulouse.

The children's home where I was sent was generally known as Moissac. It was located at 18 Quai du Port in an old house that had been unoccupied for years before being taken over by the EIF, the movement founded by Robert Gamzon in 1923. It functioned like Scout movements the world over but also strove to impart Jewish cultural values. After the Armistice in June 1940, its headquarters were transferred to Moissac in the unoccupied zone. At this point, the EIF expanded its activities to include education, culture, social welfare, clandestine rescue operations, and armed combat. It also established more children's homes, especially in the south, where there was an influx of Jewish refugees. The leadership's idea was to make Jewish youth leave the city in order to give them an education that emphasized the human and spiritual values of Judaism and to orient them toward productive professions. Several agricultural camps were also set up. By 1942, there were seven, where some 140 young people cleared the land and raised crops. Later on, it joined the armed struggle against the Nazis and the French militias known to have collaborated with the Germans. In mid-1942, as

76   Eclaireurs Israelites de France.

the danger increased, the Jewish organizations responsible for our safety – OSE and EIF – decided to establish underground systems alongside their official activities. OSE set up the "Garel Network," which undertook to care for children under the age of fourteen; EIF formed the Jewish underground "Sixieme" for older youth aged fourteen to twenty. Heinz was eleven years old at the time, and I was fourteen. We were separated because we were under the auspices of two different organizations.

Life in Moissac followed the rules laid down by the Scout Movement. Boys and girls had separate troops, but we lived daily life in close quarters. The basic group was the patrouille (patrol) – eight to ten boys aged 14 to 16 headed by one of them. We did everything together and became a sort of substitute family unit. We were expected to do most of the essential chores in the home, from peeling potatoes to washing floors. We also had some rudimentary schooling on the premises. Very few of us attended the local schools. From time to time we went on overnight hikes and camped out. We learned survival techniques – building campfires, cooking under field conditions, orienteering, and first aid. It was a way to keep very active adolescents out of trouble, instill the basic ethics of the Scouting Movement, and teach survival techniques that would shortly become very handy. Since it was a Jewish movement, we also acquired a bit of Judaism, along with various crafts.

I began learning some basic metalwork skills. Machines were scarce, and handwork was still the hallmark of a skilled craftsman. I decided I wanted to become a tool and die maker (*ajusteur* in French). I was given a file, a block of iron, and a vise, and told to get to work making perfectly flat surfaces at right angles to each other. Within days I came to hate the drudgery, so I switched to electrician, installing electric lines in rooms and wiring switches. This was a bit more varied, but we weren't given any theoretical foundation. Still, it has come in useful over the years.

One strong memory is my initiation into the Boy Scout troop. We were out camping and a fire was burning in the dark in a grassy field under some trees. We sat around, telling stories and

singing songs. At a signal from one of the boys, they all decided
to go to bed but first the campfire had to be put out. The group
of boys stood up and peed into the fire to extinguish it. I wasn't
even aware of this practice and remained sitting... unfortunately
downwind. Within seconds I was enveloped in an acrid cloud of
smoke as the burning urine turned to steam. They all had a good
laugh, and confessed that they had purposely arranged for me to
sit at that strategic spot. I was officially inducted into the troop!

The fun and games didn't last long. Within months after arriving
in Moissac, the search for Jewish children and adolescents was
so intense that a decision was made for us to go underground.

Whereas children under the age of sixteen had been allowed to
leave the camps in 1940-1941, by 1942 Vichy's Prime Minister
Laval decreed that they were to be reunited with their parents
and deported. During the last six months of 1942, 1,032 children
under the age of six, 2,557 between six and twelve, and 2,464
adolescents between thirteen and seventeen were deported
from France. None of them returned. Laval declared "Not a
single Jewish child must remain in France." Tips were received
of imminent raids. One prefect (governor) complained that "a
network of informers has gained knowledge of plans and dates of
arrests and in the process made it difficult to meet the deportation
quota."

Moissac received such a warning. The leadership sent all of its
two hundred young people on an extended "camping trip." When
the police arrived at the Center they found only the directors. The
group returned some weeks later, without those wanted by the
police. They remained in the Correze (a remote, rugged southern
region) until hiding places could be found for them.

It became increasingly clear that the shelters and homes for
young people were becoming dangerous. They were in effect
places of concentration. The EIF decided to close the institution,
provide us with false identities, and send us into hiding.

In the dead of night, some of us were taken to the attic where
we received a new identity. We were taught how to evade police
and inspectors and how to avoid getting caught. Up to this point

I had lived as Manfred Mayer (MM). Now my name was Marcel Mantes, born on February 6, 1929, in Saint Gervais d'Auvergne in the Department of Puy-de-Dome. How I was to account for my atrocious German accent when speaking French I don't remember. The Auvergne is in central France, very mountainous, and a bit behind the times. I assume they gave me an identity from there because the Maquis was very active and communications more difficult. (The word "Maquis" is Corsican for the dense brush of the hill country to which Corsicans flee when they are in trouble).

In the summer of 1942, as our parents were deported and while I was still in Aspet, the founder of the EIF, Gamzon, formed a clandestine rescue network codenamed "La Sixième" (the Sixth). It provided forged identity cards, found asylum for children and teenagers in non-Jewish homes and institutions, and smuggled Jews of all ages across the borders of Spain and Switzerland.

There were other organizations such the Oeuvre de Secours aux Enfants (OSE). I believe that my brother and cousin Ingrid were under their wing. They also created an underground network called "Circuit Garel." It sheltered and made possible the rescue of more than 5,000 children by placing them in Catholic and Protestant institutions and homes and/or smuggling them across the borders.

Everyone in France must have papers. To obtain certain papers one must first present other papers. Thus a pyramid of papers is built up through life. I was issued an identity card, food ration cards, and a birth certificate. The identity card had to correspond to a genuine registered identity, because it was only too easy for the police to make a phone call or send a telegram. Each paper had to bear the authentic stamp and signature of the authorities. To copy the stamps the various organizations had to learn to make molds. This was a massive undertaking, done at great risk. Many were executed when discovered.

I was given an ID card with all kinds of official looking rubber stampings. I was now a Catholic. My mother's name was Marie (no joke!). I forget the father's name. We spent the whole night there in the attic, getting the details right, quizzing each other, throwing questions back and forth. We had to know our new name, birth date, father, mother, without hesitation, as if our lives depended on it – and they did!

We were told how to dress, how to look nonchalant, how to play the schoolboy, how to avoid engaging in conversation with strangers. The Gestapo, in civilian clothes, was everywhere. Many of the French also reported both Jews and French Resistance fighters on the least suspicion in order to curry favor with the Germans or the Vichy police. Nobody could be trusted.

Soon after I started underground life as Marcel Mantes, I was sent to a regional boarding school in Beaumont-de-Lomagne, surrounded by French children... I was fourteen.

Since it was a regional school attended by children from neighboring communities and farms, the kids either walked home or were boarded at the school. I was boarded. Life as Marcel was not at all straightforward. I was constantly afraid – my greatest fear was discovery. I was terrified that someone would notice my German accent or the fact that I was circumcised. Unfortunately for us, circumcision in Europe was exclusively practiced by Jews, so our communal showers were a nightmare – how to appear nonchalant, but always to be ready with some excuse.

I have a feeling that the teacher was "in the know" with the people who had placed me. He introduced me to the class as a French refugee from the Alsace region on the German border, and generally tried to minimize my embarrassment when he called on me to respond to his questions. I don't remember his name, only that he was on the heavy side, blonde, and walked with a slight limp.

Farm Life

The summer vacation began soon after I arrived. The students went home, and I was sent to a farm in Montricoux. The Underground had anticipated this, and lined up a number of farms for this purpose. Once again, I was introduced as a refugee from Alsace. I don't know if they guessed my true identity – if they did, they played their parts perfectly. Never an embarrassing question. There was a farmer, his wife, and a grandmother. The farm had a couple of oxen, several cows, a lot of sheep, some rabbits, and pigeons. I was expected to help Grandma guard the sheep and do other chores. I enjoyed the work. Food was plentiful. Once a week I would cycle to the bakery to buy two loaves of freshly baked bread. The food was marvelous, Grandma really knew how to cook – always over a charcoal brazier or in a large fireplace in pots suspended over an open flame. This was old France. We had rabbits, pigeons, and even snails, but I admit that I absolutely refused to eat this last delicacy.

My main job was taking care of the sheep. There were perhaps two hundred of them to be taken out each day to pasture. Grandma showed me how it was done. She had a sheepdog that did everything she wanted, but I could never teach him to listen to me. The pasture was rather scrubby, rocky bush. As the sheep moved ahead we would cut branches and tie them into bundles, leaving them on the side of the path to be picked up later. They were used as firewood in winter and as fodder for the animals, who would nibble the now dry leaves.

Once in a while I was asked to take the three or four cows to pasture.

This was also the first time I saw the birth of a live creature. One of the cows was expecting. The farmer would go out and check progress by checking the bone structure at the rear end of the cow. He explained that the bones would become flexible and pliable when the birth was imminent. Hours later, the calf appeared, with the help of the farmer and his wife. This was better than the "birds and the bees."

Oxen did the heavy work. We had two. A big, red, older animal and a younger one. They were harnessed to a yoke and then attached to a wagon or plow. The big one didn't like me and kept trying to butt me with his long horns. I soon learned how to fasten the yoke – a heavy wooden affair just as we see in Renaissance paintings attached to the two stoic animals by long leather thongs crisscrossed in a particular pattern between yoke, horns and the foreheads of the oxen. I was allowed to do some plowing. It took some effort to keep the heavy steel plow upright and at the same time keep the ox team going in a straight line. At the end of the furrow, I would look back with great pride at the freshly turned earth, filled with wriggling worms.

Not long after, Big Red came to an unexpected end when the farmer received a mandatory requisition order to deliver one of his farm animals for slaughter to maintain the food supply. I still remember walking him with the farmer down the country road to hand him over to the authorities.

Trying to be a Good Catholic

The farmhouse was a few kilometers from the village of Montricoux. Every Sunday we traveled to church in a horse-drawn wagon. I didn't have the faintest idea how to conduct myself there. I simply copied Grandma. About a month after going to church every week, I started to get hints that I should take communion – the ceremony that signifies coming of age for Catholics. I made excuses week after week. The pressure became more intense, but I steadfastly refused. To me, it represented the ultimate denial of my Jewish identity and of my parents. It seemed like an irrevocable step. I have never forgotten the trauma and the conflict. Whenever I go into a church, those moments in Montricoux come rushing back as if yesterday. To a degree, the French clergy – from humble priests and nuns to some cardinals – did much to save thousands at their own peril. Some were denounced and killed. Their sacrifice and courage is in stark contrast with the Vatican's performance.

The eventful summer concluded and I returned to school, but not for long… It was now three years since the deportation and separation from my family. A few months after school resumed, the student body was informed that the German army would be occupying the building to quarter its troops. When we left, we were told to take any book we wanted. For some reason,

I chose the illustrated Larousse dictionary, which I still cherish today.

With the Maquis

I was taken to a Jewish unit of the Maquis, hidden in the hills. That's how I spent the remainder of the war until Liberation. Our small group consisted of teenagers (I was fifteen now) with a handful of older adults, perhaps 20-45 years old. We lived in an abandoned house, making do as best we could. The adults were very protective of the younger ones. We were not allowed to participate in their training, and certainly not in their raids. By 1944, it had become clear that Jewish survival was at stake, and we youngsters represented the only hope of renewal for the future.

We had one very close call with the Germans and their French helpers, the Milice (paramilitary Police). It was dark, about 8 o'clock in the evening, when someone spotted a long column of lights moving towards the top of the hill where we were located. The alarm was given and we girded ourselves for what was to come. We had been briefed to say we were on an outing from the Catholic Youth Organization.

The Germans arrived in trucks, set up a machine gun in the courtyard, and searched the premises. We were all assembled in the yard, silently staring at the ominous gun. They were looking for specific individuals by name. They asked questions, but we denied all knowledge. They stayed about forty-five minutes, then departed empty handed. When all was clear, some of our instructors reappeared from their hiding places in the rafters under the roof. That was one of the most dangerous situations I ever experienced during the war.

Liberation

Soon after the liberation of Paris in August 1944, many of us returned to the EIF home in Moissac, where we were delighted to meet our old friends. Some of them had been with me since Gurs and Aspet. We were relatively oblivious to many of the momentous events happening around us. We were not aware of Auschwitz or the fate of our parents. Also, since going underground two years previously and changing my identity, I had lost track of the whereabouts of my brother. When Germany surrendered in May 1945, bringing the war to an end, more children joined us, survivors of the concentration camps in Poland. One boy was assigned to my patrol. I will never forget him explaining what went on the in camps. He had pictures of the gas chambers and the crematoria. We were exposed to horror, and began to realize the fate we had escaped.

We still had no word about our parents, but we began to suspect the worst. And yet... there was still a flutter of hope that maybe both or perhaps one was still alive. They would have been 47 and 51 years old. I wrote to the International Red Cross and several other organizations asking for information. Months later, I received two certificates, still in my possession, stating that both Father and Mother had been deported from Drancy, France in August 1942 to the Auschwitz concentration camp and that no further information was available. We continued to hope against hope – perhaps the Russian troops had transferred them to Russia... but in time we reluctantly accepted reality. For many years, and occasionally even now, this uncertainty about their fate resurfaces. It seems that survivors need to see a gravestone before they can fully accept finality. In spite of our better judgment, Menachem and I thought we would find answers when we went to Auschwitz in 1990, but we only found desolation, stillness, and the disquieting rustle of aspen leaves in the wind.

Upon our return to Moissac we were billeted at Les Moulins, an impressive building erected by Pétain for the "youth of the future." By this time, I was sixteen and I became a patrol leader for eight to ten boys. Shatta and Bouli were the husband and wife team who ran the establishment with great dedication, attempting to create a home for more than one hundred young people who had been left without parents. They fed and clothed us, tried to educate us, dealt with psychological problems, and tried to help us rediscover our Jewish roots.

The policy of EIF was to prepare its charges for working life, while imparting traditional Jewish values in preparation for our move to the Jewish homeland in Palestine, which was even more vital now, in light of the devastation of the European Jewish community. Nobody consulted with us and no alternatives were suggested. As a lad of sixteen, I had a certificate attesting to the fact that I had completed my elementary school studies. Now I continued my interrupted studies to be an electrician. I envied the few children – most of them French – who took up theoretical studies.

I had lost all trace of my little brother, whom I still thought of as Heinz. Now I became increasingly concerned with what little of the family was left. I learned through the OSE that my brother had been smuggled into Switzerland. He was in a children's home operated by religious Zionists. I wanted him to join me in Moissac, but at thirteen years old, he felt strongly that he wanted to go to the Jewish homeland. In 1945, the reality of the State of Israel was still a dream. Recently we obtained a copy of our file from the OSE in Paris. They needed my permission, as the elder of the two, to let him leave, but I steadfastly refused for about a year. Eventually I changed my mind.

I also made efforts to bring my cousin Ingrid, the daughter of our uncle Moritz, to Moissac. At the time, she was ten years old. Three years earlier, when she was seven, she had been hidden with a Catholic family named Eisenreich in the town of Romans-sur-Isère (Drôme). Her false name was Marie Meyer. I went to visit her, but when I saw that she was happy where she was, I made no further attempt to remove her. Some time later, her mother's three sisters, who had immigrated to the United States before the war, insisted that she leave France and join one of them in Los Angeles. The ties of blood proved stronger than her love for her adoptive family. At the age of ten, Ingrid went to California where I saw her again seven years later.

The rescue efforts carried out by the EIF in Moissac were outstandingly successful, but they ended after the war. There was an atmosphere of discomfiture, unease and restlessness, like that of birds getting ready to migrate. Many youngsters started to make contact with relatives overseas, especially in the United States. Those born in France returned to their homes, if possible, while others left to resume their education.

In many of our discussions we came to the conclusion that all of Europe and its civilization, not just Germany, was responsible for the catastrophe we had just lived through. Many of us had no family any more, we had nowhere to go back to, and we felt no ties or loyalty to Europe. We certainly did not want to help in its reconstruction.

Out of 8,900,000 Jews within German reach, some 6,000,000 had been systematically murdered by modern industrialized methods. This was unique only because of its scale, and the vain hope that man had become more "civilized" in the twentieth century. In reality we felt it was part of the continuum of 2000 years of history, from the Roman enslavement to the first Council of Nicaea, the Spanish Inquisition, the expulsion of the Jewish population from Spain in 1492, the ghettoes in the Middle Ages, the pogroms in Russia and Poland, and the Dreyfus affair in the 1890s… No, Europe would never change.

Some time earlier, the OSE had asked me whether I had any knowledge of relatives in the United States. I remembered the names of some relatives overseas, names that had been mentioned in my parents' conversations in Germany about quota numbers. Through an advertisement in a German-Jewish weekly in New York, OSE located Adolph Heumann, the brother of the Heumann family from 10 Kirchstrasse. He wrote to me in German, inviting me to the United States. He also sent me a care package full of food, including an enormous kosher salami. For hours, our patrol room in Moissac had a constant parade of youngsters who had never seen a salami, looking for a taste. I sliced away until it was all gone.

Did I want to emigrate to the United States? My friends were separating; there was no anchor anywhere. I was torn. My brother in Switzerland had made it clear that he was adamant about going to Palestine. I decided to pay him a visit to see if

I could convince him to come with me. After four years, I had no problem recognizing my fourteen-year-old brother, who met me at Engelberg station. There was nothing I could say to persuade him to come with me to the United States. The more I talked the more obstinate he became. I finally decided to inform the OSE that I would allow him to go to Palestine while I would say yes to Mr. Heumann and go to the United States.

This is how the paths fork in our lives. Sometimes we are in control, but mostly it's an illusion; a complex series of interacting factors makes the decision for us. I stayed in Engelberg about a week, enjoying the food and the scenery. Then I returned to France and Moissac, my decision made. On the way I wondered why I had not chosen to go to Palestine? After all, I had been exposed by the EIF to my Jewish cultural heritage and many people had chosen to make their lives there.

Frankly, I am not sure exactly how my thinking evolved. It was multifaceted. Foremost was a feeling that had grown in me over the years that being Jewish was not healthy. Today, I am surprised that I can so openly admit it. But I felt that away from it all I could chose to be as much or little Jewish as I wished. It wasn't a matter of conversion but the Holocaust had shown that being identified as a Jew was a death sentence. I was going to prevent it from happening in the future, with some second thoughts in later years.

My belief in God had also been badly shattered. To my mind, He had allowed His "Chosen People" to be slaughtered in the most indescribable way, allowing Hitler, the Devil Incarnate, to triumph. I still have not made my peace. To me, the decision not to emigrate to Palestine was both a secular response to my torments and an escape.

When I changed my name, at a later stage, I am sure it was an extension of that feeling... I suppose I was still in hiding.

The other factor was the lack of roots in France. Sure I had made friends, but they were all preoccupied with their own concerns. I wasn't a French citizen. I was stateless. There is no worse feeling. It means not belonging anywhere to anyone.

Within a few weeks I received an entry permit to the United States. Ironically, the process was especially speedy in my case because I was considered to be German by the US government, and since few Germans immigrated to the United States during the war, the quota was wide open! Only one problem remained – to find a place on a ship sailing from France. The evacuation of the soldiers and their families took precedence over refugees. For a while there was a distinct possibility that my entry permit would expire before I could use it. Once again, OSE came to my aid. They managed to send me with the last soldiers leaving Europe as companion to an eight-year-old boy who was traveling to America by himself. My friends in Moissac threw me an emotional farewell party, and on December 8, 1946, when I was nearly eighteen, I left France, sailing from Europe on the *Ile de France*.

Menachem: Still Wandering

Sixth Stop: Tessin, Morcote

On November 20, 1946, I was transferred once again, this time to a refugee shelter called Morcote, in the canton of Ticino in the Italian-speaking region of Switzerland, not far from the beautiful lake and town of Lugano. Strangely enough, I hardly remember anything about it. I don't know why I was moved to this place, which was ultra-Orthodox.

Hard to believe, but at Morcote I had two religious, almost mystical, experiences. I was about fourteen at the time, my head clean shaven and adorned with two curly sidelocks. Most of my reading matter consisted of Hasidic literature and stories of demons and evil spirits. I was extremely devout.

The first experience occurred near the synagogue in Lugano. I saw a Jew with a halo, his head surrounded by bright, shining light. I have no idea who he was. I cannot explain this phenomenon, and I don't know whether anyone else saw it. The second incident is linked to a deep religious crisis in my life. I prayed to God for something, and my prayer wasn't granted. At that point, like a bolt from the blue, doubts began to gnaw at me. The questions I began asking myself continue to plague me to this day – I still have no answers. From that moment, I began to think for myself. There was nobody I could turn to, nobody I could confide in. I had to hide my inner turmoil from everyone, all the while convinced that the earth was about to open up and swallow me.

Seventh stop: Lausanne, Les Avants

On April 23, 1947 I was moved for the seventh time. This time I was sent to another refugee shelter, Les Avants, in Lausanne. I only spent eleven days here, and have absolutely no recollection of it at all; it's a kind of black hole in my memory. The only indication I have of my stay is a notation in Federal Police file No. 22838, and the reputation of the Swiss authorities for accurate records. Every one of my movements during my stay in Switzerland has been faithfully reported, filed, stamped, and sealed.

Eighth stop: Montreux, Etz Haim Yeshiva

As I said, less than two weeks later, on May 4, 1947, I arrived at the Etz Haim Yeshiva, which was situated in Montreux, in the Villa Quisina. I spent a year there, until I fled, or perhaps I was expelled – the details of my departure are not entirely clear. I didn't like the place or the learning. At fifteen I was restless, with a growing awareness of my own "self." I was becoming sick of life in institutions. I began to realize their futility and the sense of dependence on others they fostered.

I looked for ways to break away. As early as July of that year, I appealed to SHEK – the patrons and sponsors of the yeshiva – to help me obtain a passport and visa to England. I explained that I wanted to visit my aunt in London. I also maintained that I hoped to study at the ultra-Orthodox yeshiva in Gateshead, no less! A passport was issued (No. 312) as well as a permit authorizing my return to Switzerland with the status of refugee. In the end, I was not permitted to travel to England because the British Consulate refused to issue a visa. In January, I was transferred to the protection of a different organization – the Swiss-Jewish Association for Assisting Refugees (VSJF).[77]

---

77 Verbandes Schweiz. Jud. Flüchtlingshilfe, VSJF.

I left the yeshiva in May 1948. My personal file contains a great deal of correspondence about the reasons for my going. According to the yeshiva, I missed classes quite frequently. According to my version, which also appears in the file, I received permission for these absences, which were necessary while I applied for my visa to England and re-entry permit to Switzerland. One of the senior rabbis at the yeshiva wrote as follows:

> Heinz Mayer left the yeshiva at the end of April, a few days before Passover. He returned three weeks later, on May 16. After his return he continued to absent himself from classes. He comes and goes as he pleases... When I summoned him for a meeting, he informed me that he had permission from his teacher to skip classes... When I asked the teacher, he replied: "He told me he received permission from you." Heinz Mayer lied. I told him he was excused from classes until further notice. He packed his belongings and left for Lucerne...

I must point out an instructive and surprising section in the rabbi's letter:

> It is a distressing fact that refugees take liberties that Swiss people would never permit themselves. They think they are the masters and we are inferior to them... They treat us as they please...

Hard to believe, but these are the words of a distinguished Torah scholar and leading educator.

The director of VSJF responded to these comments:

> We are a Jewish relief association and it would never occur to us to make any distinction between Jews. We are not prepared to accept a situation where some are deemed more worthy than others, merely because circumstances have decreed that one person has citizenship while another does not... We were astonished to discover that you hold such attitudes and beliefs... What would you say if the press expressed views such as yours?

The letter speaks for itself.

I left the yeshiva, but I did not remove my kippa (skullcap). And yet, on the way to the train station, I went to a barbershop and had my sidelocks cut – from that day I let my hair grow longer. At first I expected the heavens to fall on me! This act represented rebellion and to some extent it also signified my new-found independence.

Ninth station: Lucerne, the Erlanger family

I traveled to Lucerne and went to live with the Erlanger family. I got to know them through two of their sons, Akiva and Haim, who were youth leaders in Engelberg and Morcote. They sometimes invited me to visit their home in Lucerne. The Erlangers were an old family of Swiss Jews with many children – eleven boys and girls – a very rare occurrence in those days, even among ultra-Orthodox families. They were good people, receiving me very warmly, especially Thea, the mother. In one of her letters she writes:

> What can you expect of a sixteen-year-old boy who has struggled for his very existence since he was a child of eight? ... He has mentioned to me, more than once, that "they treat me like a football."

Aliyah – Going to Israel

Towards the end of September 1948, I left Switzerland illegally. I traveled to the Jewish Agency office in Paris. I don't remember how I found the money for the trip or who gave me the Agency's address. I only remember how scared I was of the French police. Thirty-seven years later, in 1985, fate placed me in that same office, this time as a Jewish Agency emissary representing the State of Israel...

From the Jewish Agency in Paris I was sent to a camp for olim (immigrants to Israel), either in Marseilles or another port. Within a very short time, in the last week of September 1948, I boarded the *Atzma'ut*[78] and sailed to Israel.

Standing on the ship's deck I ripped up all my documents and certificates and watched them blow away in the wind. Heinz Mayer remained over there. I was reborn. My roots were firmly planted in the future. From now on I was **Menachem Mayer**. I was on my way home.

---

78 The *Pan Crescent*, which transported illegal immigrants, was renamed *Atzma'ut* ("independence") when the State of Israel was established, on May 14, 1948/5 Iyar 5708.

After the War
Menachem: Life in Israel

On Wednesday October 6, 1948, very early in the morning, after a voyage lasting a few days, the *Atzma'ut* dropped anchor in the bay of Haifa. It was the day after Rosh Hashanah. I felt as if I was dreaming.

At dawn, I stood on deck with another 1,050 new immigrants. We gazed at Mount Carmel as we approached the shore. We were full of hope and anticipation as we drew closer to the Promised Land. I felt I had come home. I was sixteen years old.

The State had been established a mere five months earlier. Armies of the neighboring Arab countries had invaded the new state, the War of Independence was being waged, and I wanted to be part of it.

I had no brother, relative, or friend. I was alone, but I wasn't lonely. I wanted to enlist in the Israel Defence Forces, so while still in the harbor I turned to the first Israeli policeman I saw and asked how I could sign up. He looked down at me and said: "But you're only sixteen."

After one night in the immigrants' camp at Tira, I traveled to the large Israeli city of Tel Aviv. After searching for a while, I found a job as a messenger boy with the Petra travel agency on Nahalat Binyamin Street. I rented a place to stay with the Bar Or (Breuer) family, who lived in an abandoned building in Jaffa. If I'm not mistaken, it was in the Ajami quarter. I handed over my wages to Mrs. Bar Or and in the course of time, I became part of the family. The little girls looked on me as a kind of big brother. Mr. Bar Or worked for the State Attorney. As far as I remember he was the attorney for the Tel Aviv region.

A few months later, when I was seventeen, I joined Poalei Agudat Israel,[79] preparing to enlist in the Nahal (army units that founded settlements). The new State of Israel was still in its infancy, and we all wanted to help it grow. A group of us, boys and girls, established ourselves in an abandoned schoolhouse in Masmiya (today the settlement of Mashmiya Shalom, near the Re'em intersection) and worked in the fields and orchards.

In mid-1949 the group disbanded. The more Zionistic members, myself included, moved to the Sharon area. At first we lived in a packing plant and worked in the orchards of Gan-Haim, mainly picking citrus fruits. With the approach of winter, we moved to Herzliya and settled in an abandoned packing plant in an orchard, in tents. We worked for local farmers, picking fruit, working in the fields, pouring concrete in Ramat Hasharon, and paving the coastal road near Herzliya. In those days, it was all done by hand, not by machinery. When you drive along the road, perhaps you'll remember that I also had a part in it.

We intended to save money to buy a tractor, which we could use when we started our settlement. We bought a used tractor but it soon became obvious that it was a piece of junk, costing more to repair than it was worth. Sometimes we have to learn the hard way... through experience.

In the winter of 1949-1950 it snowed heavily. Even Tel Aviv was blanketed with snow and in the orchards it was bitterly cold. When the snow melted, it flooded the tents and the packing plant. Our beds stood in pools of water. But despite the harsh conditions we didn't complain. We sensed that we belonged; we were aware that we were building our land.

In June 1950 we enlisted in the first regular Nahal battalion. We did our basic training at Camp 80. Veterans of the battalion established many settlements along the border of the time. My group, named "Shalhevet," founded Kibbutz Sha'alvim. Today it is located in the center of the country; at that time, in was on the

---

79 The emissaries of this organization, who visited the institutions where I stayed in Switzerland, were the only people I knew in Israel.

border of no-man's-land in the Ayalon Valley, opposite Latrun, which was in Jordanian hands.

Each group was expected to supply a certain percentage of its members for command positions in the IDF and I was chosen to be among them. Among my duties in the army, I commanded a platoon in Massuot Yitzhak. In June 1952, when I was released from military service, I joined the kibbutz. Living conditions were not easy. We worked by day and stood guard by night – and we were happy.

We decided to purchase a flock of sheep, and it was agreed that I would learn the secrets of raising sheep at nearby Kibbutz Gezer. For several months, I rose very early and walked the seven kilometers that separated the two kibbutzim, reversing the process at night. Who had a car? Sometimes I was lucky enough to hitch a ride. After some basic training, we bought two hundred sheep. I tended the flock on the hillsides of the Judean Plain, rifle in one hand and a book in the other... The work was arduous, the food was poor, and the hours were long; but I loved the work and the sense that we were doing something for the first time. I also enjoyed the solitude. I daydreamed; sometimes I experienced sorrow and pain.

As time passed I became an expert in sheep-rearing. I knew many of them by name or by the numbers tattooed on their ears. Did you know that each animal in the flock has its own personality? By studying their behavior patterns, I gained a better understanding of certain Biblical texts. I assisted at hundreds, if not thousands, of births. By means of cross-breeding (as Jacob did with Laban's flocks) the flock increased and the amount of milk improved noticeably.

At the end of 1955, I was sent to study farm administration at the Ruppin Agricultural School in Emek Hefer. The course lasted for nine months; the study load was intensive. These studies marked a turning point in my life – I was studying again, for the first time in many years! In effect, my formal studies had come to an end in May 1944, when I was in sixth grade. And even during the years that I attended school – what kind of conditions were there?! Different countries, different languages, different cultural frameworks: Four months in Hoffenheim, ten months in the Jewish school in Heidelberg (from Kristallnacht until our deportation from Germany), twelve months in the orphanage in Aspet, and fifteen months in Toulouse – that was the sum of my formal education! A total of forty-one months (with interruptions)! Later, in Switzerland, I spent about one and a half years in a yeshiva and hated every moment. In the other eight institutions which I attended, I never set foot in a school (actually, I have no idea why there were no classes). I always read everything I could lay my hands on, especially adventure stories. I became streetwise, I learned how to adapt to different situations, I became wary and suspicious – yet at the same time I gained faith in the future.

Now that I had tasted the fruit of the "tree of knowledge" I became aware of my ignorance, and from that moment I became a diligent student.

During that period, there were continuous incidents along the cease-fire line – infiltrators penetrated the region, *fedayeen* terrorists carried out attacks in Israel, and the IDF carried out reprisals – and the cycle would begin again. This was the normal course of our lives in all of Israel and especially in Sha'alvim. I did my reserve army duty on the kibbutz. In actual fact, we were doing army service three hundred and sixty-five days every year.

Coming in from the fields one Friday I noticed an unfamiliar girl in the kibbutz yard. That was my first glimpse of Chava. I learned later that she had come to the kibbutz to visit friends who studied with her at Horev High School in Jerusalem. When they graduated the previous year, her friends joined the kibbutz while Chava continued her studies in the School for Home Economics.

Her maiden name was Van Cleef. Her family, whose documented history goes as far back as the expulsion from the Iberian Peninsula, emigrated from Belmonte, Portugal, to Holland in 1496. In the eighteenth century, her great-grandparents moved to Germany and prospered. In 1939, her family wisely decided to leave their home in Cologne. They relocated to England, and in 1950, fourteen-year-old Chava and her Zionist parents moved to Israel.

Despite the tense situation on the borders, especially the Jordanian border near our kibbutz, we were married on October 23, 1956. Six days later, October 29, marked the beginning of the Sinai Campaign. We managed to snatch a brief honeymoon before Chava returned to Tel Hashomer Hospital, where she was completing her practical work, while I went back to commanding the guard post of Sha'alvim. In the end, it turned out that most of the fighting took place in Sinai rather than the Jordanian border.

Chava and I lived in a tiny one-room apartment (three meters by three meters!) with no bathroom, about eighty meters from the cease-fire line. There were firing slits in the outer walls of the room. We had to walk two hundred meters to take a shower, but the toilet – which was really a hole in the ground – was a mere fifty meters away! Yet despite the conditions life was good – we had no complaints. Chava worked in the kitchen and I continued herding the sheep.

Jonathan, our firstborn, arrived on December 15, 1957. Suddenly I disliked the idea that our son would be raised in a kibbutz. I wanted him to have real parents, not substitutes. In those days, kibbutz babies lived together in a children's home, and I'd had enough of institutions.

That's why we left the kibbutz in June 1958, consumed with guilt at having betrayed the kibbutz ideal. It wasn't an easy decision to make. Jonathan was six months old and we had nothing but the clothes we were wearing. At first, we stayed in the Shaffir Regional Center where we taught at the regional school. Since there was a countrywide shortage of teachers at the time, I was hired as a teacher of agriculture despite my lack of qualifications. Chava was properly trained; she taught home economics. Seven months later, we arrived at Yemin Orde, a children's village on the Carmel.

Yemin Orde was an institution where Youth Aliyah children lived and studied. We both found teaching positions there, as

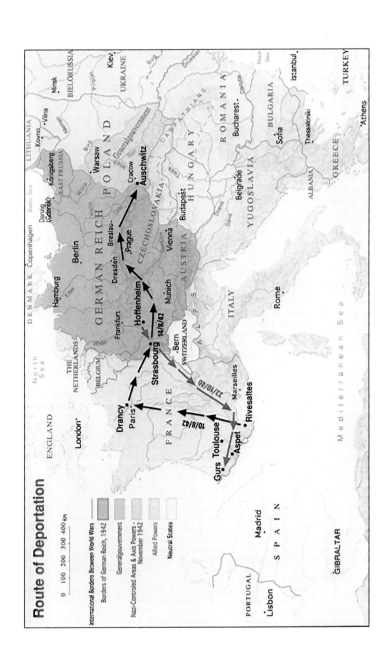

Route of Deportation

Our parents, Mathilde and Karl, 1927

Hoffenheim

The Hoffenheim Synagogue, drawing from memory, 1990

Three-year-old Heinz Mayer in Hoffenheim (front row, 7th from left)

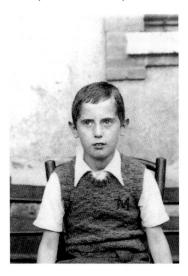

Heinz Mayer, in orphanage, 1942

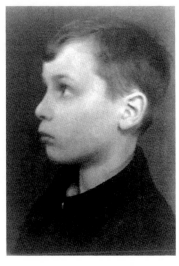

Manfred Mayer, ID card, 1938

Name: M A Y E R, Karl **Da.Nr.:** 20647 Sch.J.

BD: 29.9.94 **BP:** Frankfurth a.MNat: deutsch

Zugang: 11.11.38

Zugangsbuch des
KL.Dachau

GCC 3/61 IA/2

Record of Karl Mayer's imprisonment in Dachau. He was arrested immediately after Kristallnacht

R. F. SS

Sicherheits-Dienst

Nachrichten-Uebermittlung

Aufgenommen Monat Jahr Zeit	Befördert Tag Monat Jahr Zeit	Raum für Eingangsstempel
durch	14. Aug. 1942. 13 55	
	durch auf	
	Verzögerungsvermerk	
Nr. 16998		

Telegramm — Funkspruch — Fernschreiben — Fernspruch

IV. J SA 225 a   Paris, den 14.8.1942
He/Bir

Dringend, sofort vorlegen ! **Geheim!**

An das

Reichssicherheitshauptamt, Referat IV B 4,
z.Hd. SS-Obersturmbannführer EICHMANN, o.V.i.A.

B e r l i n

An den

Inspekteur der Konzentrationslager

in Oranienburg

An das

Konzentrationslager

in A u s c h w i t z

      Am 14.8.1942, 8,55 Uhr hat Transportzug Nr. D. 901/1
den Abgangsbahnhof Le Bourget-Drancy in Richtung Auschwitz mit
insgesamt 1000 Juden verlassen. (Darunter erstmalig Kinder)
      Der erfaßte Personenkreis entspricht den gegebenen Richt-
linien.
      Transportführer ist Stabsfeldwebel K r o p p , dem

1)   namentliche Transportliste in zweifacher Ausfertigung mitge-
geben wurde.

2)   15.8.   Mitgegebene Verpflegung wie üblich pro Jude für

3)   14 Tage.

                     I.A.

The deportation order for Transport D.901/19 to Auschwitz

Gurs Detention Camp, France

Heinz and Manfred in Hoffenheim, 1939

Manfred and Heinz in the Aspet orphanage, 1941

The children of Aspet, 1942. Heinz is in the front row, 7th from left, Manfred is in the back row, extreme left

Heinz in the Toulouse orphanage, 1943

Heinz in Engelberg, Switzerland, 1945

Manfred a.k. as Marcel (front row, center) with a group of Jewish Scouts, hiding in the forests of Southern France

Heinz in Montreux, where he studied at Etz Haim Yeshiva before making Aliya, 1947

Menachem Mayer (in white shirt) at Auschwitz with a group of young
Israelis, 1990

Menachem Mayer and Fred Raymes with their wives in Canada

Menachem Mayer and his family, 1997

Fred Raymes and his family, 1999

Memorial plague in Hoffenheim "In memory of the victims of the National Socialist Regime 1933–1945"

Letter written by mother from Rivesaltes camp, June 4 1941,
with dried flower in upper left corner

well as a place to live. In addition, I was put in charge of the agricultural teaching farm. We lived in a two-roomed Swedish style hut with – wonder of wonders – a bathroom! Such luxury! It wasn't only our "palace" and its privacy that thrilled us, but also the grass, oaks, and pine trees surrounding our home and the breathtaking scenery from our window. Our view encompassed the Carmel forest, the houses of Nir Etzion, the Atlit shoreline, and the wide blue sea beyond. And the sunsets were indescribable!

For several years, in addition to my daily routine, I studied towards a teaching diploma in natural sciences. I attended classes two evenings a week at the School of Biology in Haifa. Twice each week, I walked five kilometers down the hill to the old Haifa road, where I caught a bus to the school. Late at night I would retrace my steps. Sometimes, if I was very lucky, I caught a ride. What kept me going was the burning need to study. Also, I was fit and healthy.

Our daughter Michal was born on August 31, 1959, a few days after the birth of Fred's daughter Suzie. The place was a real paradise for children. We often walked in the forest, collecting and raising salamanders and other creatures. We learned to identify the beautiful plants of the Carmel.

In 1963, when Chava's father died unexpectedly, we moved to Jerusalem. Although Yemin Orde was a wonderful place for children, I didn't want to spend my life as a village teacher, and we wanted to live closer to Chava's mother, who was lonely. We lived in a small two-roomed apartment which was somewhat cramped with two children, but we were satisfied. I obtained a teaching position in one of the better schools in Jerusalem.

In 1964, when I was thirty-two, I was accepted as a student at the Hebrew University. I enrolled with the full realization that for the next few years I would be required to invest a great deal of effort in my studies. In 1967, I received my B.A. in education and zoology. I was very excited and moved by my achievements, because the studies were difficult, hampered by the fact that I was supporting a family and paying a mortgage at the same time. More than once I was on the point of giving up, but Chava supported me. She helped and encouraged me. Meanwhile our family continued to grow, and our son Zvi was born on November 6, 1965.

May 1967. The eve of the Six-Day War. The Egyptian army invaded Sinai and threatened to destroy the State. Abdul Nasser, president of Egypt, signed a treaty with King Hussein of Jordan and the government of Syria. The government of Israel declared a state of emergency. During the month of May, the Jerusalem Brigade was mobilized, including the 62nd regiment, in which I served. Our regiment assembled at Mt. Herzl before taking up our positions at Ramat Rachel, the southern vanguard of the city, and we waited… The battle began on June 5. The Jordanian army took over the United Nations Headquarters at Armon Hanatziv (the former British Government House) and began shelling houses in the west of the city. And so it came about that I was directly in charge of defending my home and family. This war was not conducted at long distance, with the battlefront a hundred or a thousand kilometers away. The houses were behind us, we could see their red roofs. We could hear the shells and watch them falling on the homes of our families, and we didn't know whether anyone was hurt. Our unit faced south, toward Judea. We took Bethlehem, chased the Jordanian Legion (but never encountered them), occupied the Etzion Bloc, and reached as far south as Hebron. The war was over in six days. The whole country was euphoric. My brother Fred wrote: "This is the first time I'm proud to be a Jew."

I returned home several weeks later. I enrolled in the Teachers' Seminary and one year later, in 1968, I, was appointed superintendent of natural studies for all schools in the Jerusalem area. I continued in this position until the mid-1980s. During that time I was also involved in developing new biology curricula.

In 1970, we bought our own home and moved in.

Summer 1972. One evening the telephone rang: "This is Fred. I'm in Europe. Tomorrow I'm coming to you! Meet me at the airport." We were totally astounded. Although we had written occasionally over the years, first in French, and later in English, twenty-six years had passed since last we met! I was very nervous – how would it go? I needn't have worried; it was a very successful reunion. I was surprised to find that although we parted many years ago, we have many mutual interests and similar attitudes to many things. Fred was always my "big brother" and so he remains...

Yom Kippur, October 1973. The war that broke out that day traumatized the State of Israel; its effects can be felt to this very day. This time, too, my unit was stationed in Jerusalem. In the years between these two wars I was, like everyone else, called up to reserve duty every year for thirty to forty days. Sometimes we were stationed in Gaza, other times we were on the Golan Heights. During the War of Attrition, my hearing was damaged by bombs falling nearby and afterwards I did reserve duty in the Intelligence Corps. I was discharged after serving for thirty-five years and today I still strive to contribute what I can.

In 1974, I received my M.Sc. (with distinction) in Science Teaching, from the Hebrew University of Jerusalem. At the same time I was awarded a prize by the Weizmann Institute for "developing an original biology curriculum." I had written a textbook for students aged twelve to fifteen, entitled Who am I? Human Biology. My choice of subject and teaching method were based on earlier research conducted to ascertain the topics that interest children at these ages and the teaching methods they prefer. Four years later, when I was forty-six, I completed my Ph.D. studies at the Hebrew University.

I don't know why I am driven to learn. It has not been easy; sometimes it was very hard indeed, because I always worked at the same time as I studied. Chava was always by my side, saying the right encouraging words, helping and supporting me. I began to study at a relatively advanced age. I devoted three years to evening classes and another eleven years to regular studies at University. The moral is: be careful not to determine the fate of a young person or adult by applying rigid frameworks. Provide opportunities, it's never too late.

In 1981, I was appointed Superintendent of the Jerusalem region.

In 1985, I went to western Europe as an educational attaché serving as Director of Education and Culture for the World Zionist Organization in Paris. Upon my return, I rejoined the Ministry of Education and was appointed Director of Administration and Supervisor of Special Tasks in the office of the Director General. In this capacity I have participated in UNESCO conferences on several occasions.

In July 1996, the French government awarded me the title Chevalier dans l'Ordre des Palmes Academiques (Knight of the Academic Order) for my contribution to promoting French culture. Once again, I am amazed by the vagaries of fate – this is the same France that held me and my family captive some fifty-four years ago. Or perhaps it is a different France?

I retired in November of that year. Since then, I have been working on various educational projects. I am also involved in educational counseling.

After the War
Fred: Life in the United States

My passage to the United States on the *Ile de France* cost $350, paid by Mr. Heumann and the OSE. We slept in swinging hammocks. I was seasick for a day or so, then recovered. Within five days, we entered New York's Lower Bay, early in the morning. We were all on deck, greatly excited, and anticipating the world-famous skyscrapers that spell America to all immigrants. Finally, out of the morning mist we saw lower Manhattan, slipped by the Statue of Liberty and laboriously, with a gaggle of tugs pushing and pulling, tied up at Pier 86. It was December 12, 1946. We had arrived in America.

The details have faded, but I recently discovered in the OSE archives a letter I wrote to them sixteen days after arriving:

We had to wait nine hours to disembark; first the Americans, then first class. At 4 pm the OSE representative arrived. We were the first to leave from third class. We went through immigration and customs then entered the waiting hall. There were so many people we couldn't see anybody. We called several times over loudspeakers for my "uncle" (Mr. Heumann), but there was no response. I decided to go to a telephone. The moment I was about to put a coin in someone tapped me on the shoulder and said in English: "Do you know Manfred Mayer?" It was Mr. Heumann.

We walked to the parking lot, me carrying my miserable little cardboard suitcase. I was impressed with his car – a new Chevrolet, burgundy in color. There wasn't much talking during the drive.

I didn't speak or understand English; he didn't speak French and I had suppressed my German throughout the war and had great difficulty expressing myself. At the house I was greeted by his housekeeper, Elsie – a German immigrant, Catholic, and a terrific cook. They showed me to my room, which seemed luxurious to my eyes, but I assume it was a typical bedroom. They fed me well – my weight at the time was 118 pounds!

I learned that Mr. Heumann wasn't my uncle, but that his mother was the sister of my father's mother. He was in his seventies, and had emigrated from Germany in his late teens around 1900. He had worked as a butcher and in time owned several butcher shops.

Within days Mr. Heumann asked me what I wanted to become. I said I didn't know yet, but that I was hoping to go to high school. He said, "Nonsense, you are going to be a butcher." I said I certainly did not want to be a butcher. He suggested that I go down to the store with him in the morning. So at four o'clock the next morning we drove through the dark, quiet streets of Brooklyn into lower Manhattan. I spent the day watching as he bought the meat wholesale, trucked it to his store, had it cut into appropriate pieces, and sold it to customers. All I could think of was, this is not for me; this is not how I want to spend my life. After a week came the inevitable question: "Well, what do you think? How do you like it?" I said that I had hoped to get a little more schooling, that I wanted to become an engineer. He became upset. I said that if I couldn't go back to school I would leave and do it on my own. Elsie tried to mediate between the seventy-five-year-old bull and the eighteen-year-old buck. It didn't work.

The next morning I moved into a rented room. The price was $8 a week. Then I went looking for work. I had several interviews, but no job. It was the first time in my life that I was all alone – no family, no orphanage with lots of kids, no friends, and very limited ability to communicate in English. After about a week, I found work at the Tintograph Corp., receiving the minimum wage of twenty-two dollars per week. At the same time, I began learning English at Erasmus Hall High School. To supplement my modest income I took a part-time job with Western Union delivering telegrams on weekends and at night.

I was desperate, and began asking myself why I had left the warm nest of Moissac. I even tried to enlist at an Army recruiting station. The sergeant turned me down because I could barely make myself understood in English.

Someone told me about an immigrant who had made good and might be able to help me get a better job, so I contacted Mr. Weill. He and his wife had arrived in the United States in 1938 and he became a very successful businessman. He took me to a department store near Fifth Avenue and dressed me in new clothes from head to toe. Underwear, shirt, suit, socks, shoes... I was flabbergasted and overwhelmed. This was the most moving gesture I had ever experienced – all the more meaningful because he was a total stranger and I was in dire need of a friendly connection. He also invited me into his home. Mr. Weill was never able to find me a job, but he kept encouraging me. I stayed in touch with him for many years.

I found a job in a machine shop, where my training from France came in handy. I enjoyed it, but was very concerned about speeding up my schooling so that I could start college. I attended night classes in aeronautical engineering at the Academy of Aeronautics. Tuition fees were more than I could afford but I managed to obtain a scholarship. I worked at the machine shop from eight to five, then traveled to school by subway and bus to study from six to ten. I also moved closer to the school. It was quite a grind, but with my goal clearly in mind I put my head down and persevered. Later, I switched to studying during the day and working at night at the insistence of my draft board because of the Korean war then in progress. I graduated in 1952 – a time of jobs aplenty. Nine months before graduating, we were already being wooed by the giants of the aerospace business: Boeing, Lockheed, and others. Business was booming, technical help in short supply. The sky was the limit. At the graduation ceremony, I read my award-winning paper on the subject of the "Boundary Layer." I had a strange feeling of awe, pride, and loneliness, that this young refugee only five-and-a-half years off the boat was speaking to a crowd of several hundred, when not too long ago he couldn't put together three words in English.

I graduated on August 1, 1952, fourth in a class of twenty-five. I had five job offers, and accepted the position offered by North American Aviation as a thermodynamicist in their engineering department. The decision was very simple; I had read and dreamed about California for some time, it was the state of the future, of sunshine, of young people; it was new; it was exciting; it was "it." The fact that my cousin Ingrid lived there also helped. I left New York with no regrets.

Citizen Raymes

There was just one fly in the ointment: I was still not a citizen of the United States. All the offers were contingent on being able to obtain a Defense Department security clearance, so citizenship was essential. On June 2, 1952, I became a citizen at the age of twenty-three. I was stateless no more. My pride and joy cannot be described. I have never since missed voting in an election. It's my way of reaffirming my love and faith in this country.

The judge asked if I wanted to change my name, no charge. I said yes. First to go was Manfred – it was too German. The abbreviation Fred was natural, then for reasons only a psychologist would understand I picked Frederick, which I could have spelled with a "c." For reasons beyond me, I selected the very German "ck." I suspect I didn't want to lose my roots, that tenuous thread that holds us to the past. The family name, Mayer, was a more emotional issue. I still carried the emotional scars of being Jewish in Europe and I continued to conceal my Jewish identity. I was aware of antisemitism in American corporations and had seen "No Jews Allowed" signs on Long Island golf courses in the 1950s. I scrambled the letters of my surname and eventually came up with Raymes. It sounded innocuous, vaguely familiar, but I have never run into another Raymes.

Do I have any regrets? Not really. Would I do it again? Probably not. Times are different, American society has changed. I don't feel quite so self-conscious about my Jewishness. I feel more secure.

Immediately after graduation I drove to Los Angeles and began my new job at North American Aviation, working on many of their aircraft programs. Problems involving the internal aerodynamics of these aircraft included cooling, heating, and propulsion. Work was intense; I loved the laboratories and the wind tunnels and was an avid learner. Word got around that I spoke French and I got to meet several high company executives when representatives of the French company Sud Aviation visited Southern California. All the while I continued to go to evening school for the next ten years to obtain both a Bachelor's and a Master's degree. I also found time for romance, having met my future wife, Diane, at Hillel House at the university. We were married in August 1953, and my cousin Ingrid, then seventeen years old, was at the wedding.

In 1954, close to the end of the Korean War, the United States Army drafted me. After basic training with a military speciality of Aeronautical Engineer, I was attached to the Engineering Corps. Because I had only eight weeks of basic training, I was the lowest private in the army and there was more kitchen duty than engineering. I appealed to my direct superiors on more than one occasion to be given a posting more suited to my qualifications, but it did no good. Then I decided to circumvent the bureaucracy by applying for a transfer to Redstone Arsenal in Alabama. The transfer was approved within two weeks – to join the group of engineers working under Werner von Braun, the German scientist of Nazi V-2 rocket fame, who headed the United States missile program.[80] This just goes to show that if you don't have

---

80 During that time, nuclear development in the United States was rapidly forging ahead. The success of the USSR in sending missiles into space spurred on the United States to invest vast resources in this field. They even recruited German scientists – headed by Werner von Braun – to develop important projects, using the experience they had gained in Germany during the war.

connections you need resourcefulness or *hutzpa* (or better yet, both).

Arriving at Redstone Arsenal I presented myself to Dr. Geisler, the close personal assistant to von Braun. He spoke English with a heavy German accent. I was in US Army uniform, and I debated whether to reveal my personal history, but chose not to. I was not looking for false sympathy, nor the usual denials from the Germans that they saw nothing, heard nothing. I described my professional experience, and he told me about the work at Peenemunde – the German site where they developed the V-2 rockets used in the Second World War. He went on to describe the terrible suffering he had endured: "Imagine, in all that time I only ate four little squares of chocolate!" he told me. All this, while the crematoria in Auschwitz blazed non-stop, and I myself had been in hiding... I didn't utter a single word. I was assigned to the aeroballistics laboratory with a group of American civilian and military engineers working on the Jupiter rocket, a cousin to the V-2. I had a hand in the design for the launch mechanism of the Explorer I satellite, created as a response to the USSR's launch of Sputnik. During the entire time I spent in the plant, I kept my distance from the Germans. As soon as I was discharged two years later, I returned to my former place of work.

Besides working forty-five hours a week I continued studying at night. In 1959, I was awarded a science and engineering degree, and in 1964, I received an M.A. in business administration. On August 26, 1959, our daughter Suzie was born; our son David was born two years later, on July 17, 1961.

My involvement in the space program grew rapidly. I became restless. I aspired to a more challenging position in the field, something that would enable me to express more breadth of vision. I left NAA for the deputy directorship in the laboratory of the Aerospace Corporation. This company acted as consultant to the US Air Force in all that pertains to space and missiles. I worked in my field of expertise: counteracting the heating effects generated by the high speeds of spacecraft re-entering the earth's atmosphere. Of particular interest were spacecraft that had the ability to maneuver on return to the earth's atmosphere instead of traveling on a pure ballistic path. Ten years later, this led to my intense involvement with the space shuttle. These are the subjects that occupied me for twenty years. Two patents were issued by the US Patent Office bearing my name for the design of spacecraft on re-entry into the atmosphere.

At some stage, I became aware that I was involved in developing nuclear weapons, their protective devices, and methods to improve their lethal efficiency. It disturbed me, so I requested a transfer. I know that it is merely an illusion to think that I could disassociate myself from weapons development by transferring. In actual fact, we're all involved in it, starting from the taxpayers at the bottom of the pyramid, even if it's not our finger pushing the button. But my more direct participation troubled me, and I preferred to focus on another area. From then on, I took part in developing information-gathering equipment for reconnaissance satellites.

North American Aviation asked me to come back to work for them after they won the competition to build the Command/ Service module for the Apollo program. There I led a group involved in astronaut protection from space radiation and solar flares. As the engineering of Apollo neared its end, the company became concerned with what was to follow this 25-billion-dollar program and the massive employment and industrial infrastructure it had created. I was asked to lead a group to study alternatives. I spent some time in Washington on loan to NASA. Out of these studies came the recommendation to go on to create a reusable maneuverable spacecraft that could go into space repeatedly – the space shuttle.

At the height of its activity, NASA itself employed 36,000 workers, with another 411,000 more employed through subcontractors. It had a budget of six billion dollars per year, representing one percent of the Gross National Product of the United States. America's image as a technological superpower was greater than ever; we had won the space race against the Russians, but tough questions were being asked in Congress: What was the justification for spending vast sums of money on space? Would the money not be better spent on building more schools and hospitals and combating poverty? We had to convince Congress that it was necessary to continue developing the space program. The space shuttle was the outcome. I don't claim that I invented the space shuttle, but there is no doubt that for ten years I made a decisive contribution to its development.

In 1972, Grumman Aerospace Corporation on Long Island's east coast offered me the position of deputy director in charge of the space shuttle proposal. I was still young (forty-one) and ambitious, so after eighteen years, I left my beloved California, albeit with some trepidation. I led several thousand engineers for more than two years studying space shuttle alternatives as the original ideas became too costly. I worked for Grumman for the following twenty years. Some years later, I was appointed vice president in charge of international markets.

From 1974 to 1992, I traveled a great deal – to as many as 42 countries, including Israel.

In 1980, my wife Diana became ill. Her disease became ever more severe, leading to near-paralysis. I was fortunate to find a wonderful young woman named Lydia from the Caribbean island of St. Lucia to help me take care of her until her death in 1993. In 1992, I retired after working forty years in the defense aerospace industry. I built a house in a small, nearly forgotten town at the end of Long Island. I had sailing in my blood, and this was my opportunity to enjoy the wind.

In 1994, I moved to Sarasota, Florida. I am involved in the community, spending my time in volunteer work: counseling businesses, visiting the aged, advising the local authority, and lecturing on the Holocaust at local schools. I also found time to marry Lydia, and to stay in close touch with daughter Suzie and son David and the five grandchildren.

PART III

Reunited at Last

Closing Circles

Auschwitz, 1990

Fred: Czechoslovakia and Poland had finally broken free of their long servitude to the Soviet Union. They began to denounce Communism, taking their first hesitant steps towards a free market economy. During that period, I was deeply involved in international trade. Strategic trade agreements between large companies were very much in vogue, and I decided to look into aerospace industry possibilities in Czechoslovakia and Poland. The idea of going to Poland filled me with dread, because I knew I couldn't leave Poland without going to Auschwitz. I also knew I couldn't do it alone. So I called Menachem: "Let's meet in Warsaw three days from now and go to Auschwitz together." My brother immediately agreed.

Menachem: Actually I didn't want to see Auschwitz; in fact I didn't want to go at all. But I knew this journey was very important to my brother, so I agreed to meet him.

Fred: For forty-five years I had lived with the knowledge that one day I would have to deal with it – I needed to see for myself the place where Mother, Father, and other family members met their end. I knew there was no similarity between what happened to them and what we would see. As time passed, my feelings of guilt grew stronger and what began as an urge became an obsession; I had to see the place, smell it, hear it, walk where they had walked. I hoped in this way to rid myself of my guilt for not having been there with them.

I met my brother in Warsaw. The day was cold and gray. It was raining as we visited the Jewish quarter. Nothing much remains, apart from a few scattered traces where residential housing is going up. We saw the depressing Socialist-Communist-style monument erected to the memory of a Jewish community of some three million souls, which was almost entirely wiped out.

We took the train to Cracow and spent the Sabbath there. We visited the ancient, beautifully preserved Jewish quarter with its synagogue – but it was ghost-ridden.

On Sunday morning, we hired a taxi to Auschwitz, some forty kilometers away. Road signs indicated that we were getting close. We traveled on, silent and withdrawn. Whenever the car crossed a railway line, thoughts and associations swirled through our minds. I'm glad that I had Menachem with me; I couldn't have done it by myself.

Auschwitz concentration camp is made up of two areas, one kilometer apart – Auschwitz and Birkenau. We arrived at Auschwitz, entering through the gates, over which are inscribed in German the words: "Work Makes You Free." This is where they carried out the medical experiments and the hangings – on meat hooks – so that all should see and fear. The Auschwitz camp was not big enough to carry out mass murder on an industrial scale, so they built Birkenau nearby.

Today visitors are shown a film made by the Russian army as they entered the camp. Mountains of shoes, suitcases, eyeglasses, and other items are displayed in a kind of museum. We didn't want to view these horrors. We walked to Birkenau, to the place where our parents were killed, the place to which my nightmares have carried me, over and over. As we walked the railroad tracks converged; I could almost hear the shriek of engines. Every day countless freight trains traveled these tracks. They came from all over Europe, carrying their human cargo. What thoughts passed through the mind of the locomotive engineer?

We marched bravely on, not speaking to each other. Each was lost in his own tortured world. The rails looked rusty, but in excellent condition. We walked through the entrance. I visualized the steam locomotives making their way slowly now, the plume of smoke temporarily flattened as it passed under the portico. I could hear the brakes screeching – the end of the line was a quarter of a mile away. Yellow dandelion blossoms shone between the rails and rocks; I didn't think it right for any flower to bloom in this place. I picked up two rocks, stumbled on in a fog. We had reached the end of the line.

Alongside the rail line was a gravel roadway. This is where I had read that the people were off-loaded after days of horrendous travel, told to line up and approach the table step by step, toward the spot where the likes of Dr. Mengele made their "Selection." Right, Left: live a while, die now... I could see in my mind's eye the shuffling humanity, the guards, the snarling Shepherd dogs, the whips.

Not far off to the left we saw a pile of concrete rubble. We headed for it. It was one of the gas chambers blown up by the Nazis to cover up the evidence, just before the Russians arrived.

A thoughtful sign warned in five languages: It is dangerous to walk on the ruins. The ultimate of ironies. Nearby was another sign: "Pits for human ashes."

We had had nightmares for years, now we had seen, if not experienced, what our Father and Mother, Uncles Moritz and Emanuel, Aunt Alma, and Cousin Helmut had to suffer.

As we stood there in our reverie, numb, thinking of their last agonizing moments, we heard singing from afar. Away in the distance, coming through the portico I could see waving flags and marching youngsters. As they came closer, I could make out the blue and white of Israeli flags waving in the wind, carried by perhaps fifty young people. Menachem explained to me that these were Israeli high school students about to graduate. Every year a trip is organized for these young adults, many of whom are descendants of survivors, to visit the concentration camps in Poland. Menachem had been asked by the Ministry of Education, for which he worked as a director, to address the group since he would be in Poland. Six students, one for each million murdered, clambered up the pile of concrete, each with flag flying, all singing Hatikva, the Israeli national anthem.

It struck me that they were saying: "We are here and we won in spite of what you Germans tried to do." But in truth, the loss for the Jewish community and for all of humanity is immeasurable. Not only the six million dead, but all the creativity they could have contributed to society. Apart from that, there are those who survived the camps and their children – scarred for generations to come.

Each person then read an unending list of names of persons murdered in Auschwitz. I stood aside and watched in amazement. Menachem stepped forward and made a short speech in Hebrew to the group. Later I asked him to translate it for me. This is what he said:

On August 14, 1942, at 8:55 in the morning, freight train no. 901/19 left Drancy concentration camp in France carrying 1,050 Jews. The documents showed that they were old people, women, men, and more than one hundred children. According to the records the train traveled to Auschwitz-Birkenau. The entire transport went through the selection process: one hundred and fifteen men were sent into the camp, all the others went directly to the gas chambers. By the end of the war only one man remained alive of that trainload. Our parents were among the passengers. This morning, on my way here, I wrote down a few words:

Why?
Why do the birds chirp? Why does the grass grow? Why do I remain, of a million and a half Jewish children?
Why did you disappear. Almighty God?
I am angry with You and I will continue arguing with You as long as I live.
Why?
And yet – *Yitgadal Veyitkadash*…[81]

Auschwitz-Birkenau, May 6, 1990, 11 Iyar 5750.

---

81 The first words of the Kaddish, the Jewish mourner's prayer.

That's how the pilgrimage to Auschwitz ended. We followed the path of suffering, and then flew directly to Germany. We were going to Hoffenheim on a joint quest for our roots; perhaps our encounter with the new generation of Germans would also help heal our wounds.

Hoffenheim, 1974

Menachem: This would not be my first visit to Germany. In 1974, after a great deal of hesitation and soul-searching, I joined a delegation of educators on a study mission to Germany. On the one hand I felt revulsion – what was Germany to me? But on the other hand, I was caught up by silken threads of enchantment – I was curiously and strongly drawn to return to my hidden roots, perhaps to discover my stolen childhood.

One day I left the delegation and traveled to Hoffenheim, drawn by an irresistible, almost magnetic force. The following excerpts are taken from a letter I wrote home afterwards:

> The train arrived in Heidelberg at 10:00, right on time. This passion for punctuality is almost a sickness. It is Germany's blessing and curse. While still on the train, I asked the conductor about train times. He pulled a fat volume from his satchel, and methodically and carefully he began listing the required information. He copied the train schedule word for word, repeating everything on each succeeding line, even when he could have put ditto marks.
>
> I told him that what he had written was sufficient, but he dug in his heels: "Sie haben mir ein Befehl gegeben!" said he. "You have given me an order!" You see, they haven't changed. No sense of personal initiative, no deviation from orders.

From Heidelberg I traveled to Hoffenheim, to the village center. The heart of my childhood world had not changed, except in its dimensions: everything had shrunk... I wandered through the streets, very agitated. Then I walked into a forest on the edge of the village – one of the forests in which we used to walk on Shabbat and holidays. I recognized the scents and the colors instantly. Suddenly I longed for the world of yesterday, that is no longer. I returned to the village, and tried to talk to five of the townspeople. Four of them "had forgotten" or "didn't know." One old woman was working in the yard, opposite the spot where the synagogue stood until it was destroyed on Kristallnacht. She didn't know the Mayer family – never heard of them. I went into a shop, opposite the house we lived in until we were deported, and talked with the owner.

He remembered our family, the names of our parents, and even the children's names, but he couldn't quite decide whether I was Manfred or Heinz! He was most surprised to see me. "When did you emigrate to America?" I replied, "We emigrated to Auschwitz." Another woman I spoke to said, "Yes, I remember." She recalled names. No expressions of sorrow or regret. Nothing. Nothing. I suppose that's also a way of dealing with it. I went to the house at 10 Kirchstrasse and after much hesitation I knocked at the door, thinking maybe I'd find some object, a small detail, a memory of what had been. The door was opened by an old woman. Before I could even open my mouth she said: "I spent a lot of money fixing up this house…" I had barely taken two steps inside when the entrance door behind me opened. There stood two middle-aged men wearing peaked caps, of the kind favored by the Nazis. (I assume that the shopkeeper summoned these thugs, warning them that "some Jew is wandering around the village. He's gone into the house where he used to live.") They simply stood there looking at me. I left the house immediately, and the two of them followed me until I reached the center of the village. The owner of a souvenir shop was the only one who showed any emotion. She burst into tears and apologized – she was the only one who behaved like a human being. At the time, she had been seventeen, and she remembered how we were arrested and deported. When she asked why I had come to Hoffenheim I replied: "I came to see whether the earth had opened up and swallowed you all." Later I was sorry that I had said those harsh words to her, of all people. I left the place, and assumed I'd never go back.

But twelve years later I did go back, when I decided to collect testimony and documents. And I returned a third time in 1990, with my brother Fred, after our visit to Auschwitz.

Hoffenheim, 1986

Menachem: This time Chava and I were the guests of Matthias Uhlig, a young Protestant pastor. I met Mr. Uhlig for the first time in Paris, when I was with the delegation. He came to interview me and explore our history and that of the local Jewish community. He was helping a colleague, who was writing a research paper on "The Hoffenheim Jewish community from 1914 to 1945." He actually helped me far more than I helped him by supplying anecdotes of our long-forgotten school days.

Now, in June 1986, Chava and I returned to my birthplace. We traveled to the town of Waibstadt, because the regional Jewish cemetery was nearby. Fred had told me that our grandparents' graves were there. When I went in search of my roots, these graves assumed great importance for me. They proved that I wasn't some kind of virtual creature – I had a past and a history. The cemetery is located on a forested hillside. Apart from the gentle whisper of the leaves not a sound could be heard. For centuries, the Jews of the area came here to bury their dead; there were many headstones sunk into the ground. Impossible not to feel a sense of awe. We found the grave of our father's parents – their names, in Hebrew and German, were carved into the stone. Now I also knew who I was named for – the father of grandmother Klara, who died in 1926.

Hoffenheim, 1990

Menachem: After that visit to Auschwitz we decided to close the circle with a visit to Hoffenheim. Fred had no connections with Germany, but I had a few, especially with several pastors of the Protestant church. Matthias Uhlig, the local pastor, knew we were coming. He waited for us in his home. For our meeting, he had invited some of the worthy local folk – "Guten (good) Hoffenheimers," as he put it.

We drove into Hoffenheim together for the first time in fifty years. We headed straight for the Protestant church.

Introductions were made. An attractive thirty-five-year-old schoolteacher was there, full of questions. A man about our age claimed he had been in that first year elementary school class with Fred. The twenty-five-year-old seminary student, Ludwig Streib, amazingly enough, had just completed his thesis, entitled The Jewish Community of Hoffenheim 1918 to 1945. We were fascinated.

He handed us a copy and proceeded to ask questions to clarify issues he was unsure of. Laboriously, in German mixed with English, we answered as best we could. He explained that he had had problems getting the information together. This included threats from local ex-Nazis who preferred to let sleeping dogs lie. Significantly, the group did not include any locals who had been adults fifty years earlier. Mr. Streib's thesis is a fascinating history of the community. Most facts were new to us. Not only had he found pictures of Fred and me in first grade, but he had records of our performance at school. Amazing what they will save.

Fred: The pastor asked if we wanted to take a walk in the village. He said one of his ninety-plus-year-old parishioners had asked that we stop by, after our visit – it was announced at the church service. She greeted the "Mayer boys" with joy, explaining that she was the wife of the shoemaker, long deceased. She claimed to remember our father, Karl, very well. She informed us that Father used to ask her husband to cut a hole into his shoe at the strategic location where it put pressure on his corns. It's true that he had extremely painful corns that gave him no end of difficulty. I was overwhelmed by this very personal detail and embraced her.

We also walked to the local cemetery, where we had been told that after years of animosity, the village had finally agreed to install a memorial to the victims of the Nazis. At the rear of the cemetery, on a wall next to a monument commemorating the fallen soldiers of 1870 and the First and Second World Wars, was a brass plaque inscribed with the words: In memory of the victims of the Nationalist-Socialist regime, 1933-1945 decorated with a seven branched candelabra and also, to our consternation, with several crosses. They asked for our reaction. I was too reserved to tell them what I thought, but Menachem said in German: "How can you even think of equating the Jewish agony under Nazism with the Christian experience?" They were apologetic and the pastor said it was the most they could get approved by the local authorities.

Menachem: It appears that the general public and the town council do not approve of his interest in the town's Jewish history. He has even been threatened on more than one occasion. Apart from a handful of youngsters who support him, he said, he is alone in the system. But these young people are also not willing to bear the guilt of their parents any longer. They seek to open a new page, by forgetting and glossing over the past. And so, unwillingly, we parted...

Fred: Yes, the scars run deep; with some things, we will never come to terms. We stopped at a number of other spots in the village that held memories for us, then said our goodbyes. We ended up in Weinheim, where Menachem had agreed to have dinner at the home of another pastor with whom he was in contact, Pastor Lohrbacher. His wife, aged about forty, wore a prominent Star of David. When I asked her why, she said that she identifies very strongly with the Jewish people and goes frequently to Israel. She feels her generation has to do all it can to make up for the deeds of the earlier generation. Her compassion and torment had a profound effect on me. I knew that one should not judge all by the deeds of some, even if they are the majority. Here was proof.

I trace my own healing and more sympathetic understanding of the Germans of that generation to my better comprehension of the enormous burden they carry for their elders. How the younger generation must suffer, even though they are not responsible, as they travel the world, references to the Holocaust being so pervasive. Being identified as a German must be like the mark of Cain: answerable for the genocide of a People, the murder of millions...

Let us not visit the sins of the fathers on the children.

There by the Cedars

Lyrics: Y. Peled
Hebrew: A. Pompiansky
English translation: S. Berman
Melody: Folksong

At the place where the cedars kiss the clouds,
Where the waves of the Jordan spill out in a torrent,
The place where my father's bones are buried,
Where the blood of the Maccabees saturates the earth,
On the shore of the blue sea, there is everything I cherish,
There is my land, the land of my fathers.

I was plucked from there at a time of cruel power,
And hurled in fury to a strange land –
My heart remained in Zion,
I look eastward, my eye is drawn there,
My face is turned to the east while I pray,
To return to the land of my fathers.

And if God's hand will suddenly smite me,
So I die an untimely death in a strange land,
Then lower me into my grave, my brothers,
Turn my face to the east as I lie in my grave!
And place my head towards Zion –
Facing the land of my fathers.

Epilogue

The Mayer-Raymes Family Gathering

The following, by way of background, is an introduction to one of a handful of life experiences any one individual is could experience. The fact that two nuclear families consisting of twenty-nine people, living 5,000 miles apart, were able to meet at ground zero, so to speak, in Hoffenheim in Germany, our birthplace and from where we were deported, is at the heart of this story.

How did it come about? Who made it possible? What was accomplished?

Shortly after the first edition of our book was published, Menachem sent a copy of the book to Pastor Uhlig in Germany. Pastor Uhlig was at one time Pastor of the Hoffenheim Protestant Church. Menachem has known him for many years and Pastor Uhlig insisted it was imperative to publish the book in German. He asked for our agreement and within a few months he informed us that he had found someone to provide the funds as well as a top-notch English-German translator. When we inquired who was providing the funds he said "the Hopp family." We realized, we had written about someone called Emile Hopp the local SA Commander and Fred's first grade school teacher, who was sentenced after the Second World War to eleven weeks in prison by a German court for destroying the Hoffenheim Synagogue. Was this in fact the same family?

To make a long and amazing story shorter, the answer was 'yes'. Emile Hopp was the father of three children: Karola, Ruediger and Dietmar. When we were deported in 1940, Karola was eleven years old, and the brothers were two and one, respectively. As adults, the brothers worked for IBM. In time, Dietmar left IBM and became one of the founders of SAP, the prominent German software company. Up to this point we had no contact with the Hopp family, but Pastor Uhlig assured us they were anxious to see the book published.

Menachem and I agonized over the issue of whether we should accept the Hopp offer to finance the book, particularly when we received some indication that they would like to see some changes made concerning their father. We responded in the negative, saying it was not possible; changes to the book wouldn't be right, and would return to haunt us. They agreed to proceed with the publication of the book as is.

That left the matter of the Hopp family history. We concluded that since the brothers were very young children, we would not want them to suffer for the 'sins' of their father. It would not be just on our part to hold the second and third generations responsible for the Nazi crimes. We agreed to go ahead. From mid-2003 innumerable letters, faxes and e-mails were exchanged weekly between Dossenheim, Achern, Jerusalem and Florida, to coordinate the ever-mounting details including the English-German translation by Frau Franke.

In the fall of 2004, Fred was informed that the Hopps were vacationing in Naples, Florida, close to where he lives, and that they were thinking of getting in touch with him to make contact between the families. In November 2004, he and Lydia met both Dr. Ruediger Hopp and his sister Karola Muehlburger in Sarasota. When Ruediger (we are now on first-name terms) stretched out his hand that first time and said, "Thank you Mr. Raymes for being willing to shake our hands," we were overcome with emotion and embraced them. There were 60 years of agony and pain in that word and all four of us knew it.

During lunch we spoke about many things. Lydia carried on a conversation as best as she could with Karola, whose English is limited. At some point, Ruediger expressed the hope that we would come to Germany for the book launch; he also informed us that he and his sister had decided to sponsor and arrange for a Memorial Plaque to commemorate the deported Hoffenheimer Jews, listing the names of those murdered in Auschwitz and the survivors. They hoped that both the book and the plaque's unveiling could take place at the same time, in the fall of 2005.

After lunch, Karola handed us an eight-page letter she had written in German the day before, because she felt she could not sufficiently express her feelings in English. What follows is a rough translation.

Naples, November 15, 2004

Dear Mr. Raymes,

I am awaiting our meeting on Thursday with great trepidation and deep emotions. I will write to you in German and not in my limited English, to be sure to express my feelings and memories correctly. I have only a few recollections: there are the two young boys going home from the train station. I see them often when I am looking out the window of our apartment on Banhofstrasse. They are always well dressed and create a handsome impression, in contrast to the other village boys.

I also remember your aunt, Ms. Elsa Mayer, a lovely quiet woman. She came to us once a week to sell us challah bread. She carried the bread in a small basket, which was covered with a white linen cloth.

My mother and I were very sad when she couldn't come anymore. The local Nazi leader, who lived in the apartment below ours, behaved furiously because Jews had entered our home. My mother always said, "She (Ms. Mayer) needs the small income," but there wasn't enough courage to listen to the heart.

November 9, 1938, is a depressing memory for me. Via my grandfather's telephone, my father received the order to destroy the synagogue early that morning. My mother was very unhappy with this crime, and was convinced for a long time that God would punish our family.

I don't remember the day of your deportation very well; I only know that we were told that the Jews were going to a country where all the Jews would be together. I was told the same about a Gypsy family that disappeared.

Only after the collapse of the Nazi regime did we become aware of the indescribable horror that had happened. This became a horrifying reality not to be forgotten.

After I finished high school and during my teaching career, I had close connections with the Evangelical Sisterhood of Mary in Darmstadt. The sisterhood called for penance for the terrible guilt that our people took upon themselves. The nuns were full of love for the people of Israel and they succeeded to awaken this love in us too... I was so ashamed of my father's past activities that, to this day, I never even told my own children about them. Shortly after I returned from Naples, my grandson accidentally found the correspondence between you, your brother and my brother Ruediger. At his insistent request, I finally had to tell him about the past.

My family asked me to participate in the financing of the memorial plaque in Hoffenheim, and of course I am willing and happy to do so.

In Naples, I finished reading your book and I was deeply touched and moved by it.

Since my childhood, the book of Psalms has been my favorite prayer book. During my entire life I have thought of how the Jewish people in persecution and in the death camps recited the Psalms and asked the question, "Why did You, God, allow these horrifying things to happen?" I tried to find an answer to this question in Dorothee Sölle's book *Christ the Representative: An essay in theology after the Death of God.*[82]

I want you to know how happy I am that I could contribute to the memorial plaque in Hoffenheim, a small token of my deep sorrow for the past events.

With sincerity,
Yours
Karola Muehlburger (née Hopp)

---

82 Sölle, Dorothee, *Christ the Representative: An essay in theology after the Death of God,* (Philadelphia, Fortress Press, 1967).

This letter from Karola, and Ruediger's empathy, fully convinced us of the Hopp family's sorrow and their own anguish over the past. It erased any reservations we may have had to cooperate with them. In the book we speak with some indignation of a previous memorial plaque in the town, which is well-hidden in the local cemetery. We expressed the hope that the text and location of the new proposed memorial plaque would be more fitting. Dr. Hopp asked us to suggest appropriate wording. We did so and it was accepted. We therefore agreed to the idea of a memorial and to attend the unveiling. All this took place while we were wondering among ourselves what motivated the Hopp family, in light of their prominence, to step forward so many years later, open old wounds and re-expose their father's past in the presence of the media. We asked Ruediger that question; he answered in a straightforward manner:

> When we learned as recently as 2003 from your book that some Hoffenheimer Jews had survived the Holocaust, the Hopp family decided to take some measures to do what we could as the circumstances presented themselves, i.e., publication of the book, the Memorial Plaque to the deported, and sponsoring an Israeli-German youth exchange program. All was aimed at reminding us of the past and educating new generations to prevent a recurrence in the future.

Matters moved with speed; Menachem reviewed the book's German galleys several times; Ruediger informed us formally that his brother would like the entire family to come over; they would take care of the airfare, hotel and food for our four days in Heidelberg. Through the magic of innumerable e-mails we got him to define 'family'. Answer: first, second, and third generation.

Untiring Pastor Uhlig did the work of coordinating the countless details with Ruediger; not least was the wording and location of the memorial plaque. It took some doing to get the authorities to agree to place it at the entrance of Hoffenheim's City Hall, the very spot from which we were deported.

Arrival in Germany

We had agreed that all the members of our family would gather from the four corners of the earth and meet in Heidelberg on Thursday, September 1, 2005. What follows is a day-by-day summary of events culminating on September 4 with the unveiling of the memorial plaque.

Thursday, September 1, 2005. We all checked in at the Heidelberg NH hotel. We had forgotten that filmmakers would be present. As we stepped out of the taxi, cameras and microphones surrounded us and they would follow us for nearly the entire duration of our stay. That evening, dinner was served in a private dining room and all the family members were introduced to each other.

Friday, September 2, 2005. After breakfast, we boarded the bus, charted by Dr. Hopp, for a visit to the city of Worms. Pastor Albrecht Lohrbacher, who acted as our guide, accompanied us; he provided a running commentary as we drove along. Worms was one of the oldest Jewish communities in Germany, dating back to Roman times.

We looked at the Cathedral and went to the Judengasse (Jews' Lane) and the Synagogenplatz (Synagogue Square). We saw Rashi's house where, it is assumed, the former teaching house (Bet Midrash) once stood. It was in this teaching house that Rashi, the eminent Jewish scholar, once studied, circa 1060. We then descended to the ritual bath (mikve), dating from 1189. Most of our time was spent at the ancient Worms Jewish cemetery, which is Europe's oldest preserved Jewish cemetery. Many eminent scholars are buried there.

From Worms we toured the 'Wine Strasse,' a region of vineyards with romantic and prosperous villages. We returned to the hotel and prepared for Shabbat. We welcomed the Shabbat (with the Kabbalat Shabbat prayer service), and all the women lit Shabbat candles.

At the first Shabbat family dinner, twenty-nine of us sat around the long dining table; the very first time we were ever together as one family. Our guests of honor were Pastor Lohrbacher and his wife Ulrike.

The meal was delicious, doubly so, because the Hopps had amazingly arranged to have kosher food delivered, all the way from Frankfurt, so that everyone would feel comfortable.

Saturday September 3, 2005. We were on our own, no formal plans; everyone was anxious to tour the old city of Heidelberg, famous for its 12th century university and its castle overlooking the Neckar river.

Fred: I looked avidly for old landmarks from my school days 65 years ago, but only recognized a few. We stumbled on a vacant lot in the old city where the Heidelberg Synagogue once stood. Markers placed by the city explained its fate on Kristallnacht and that of the Heidelberg Jewish community who were deported with us to Gurs detention camp in France. Suddenly the tourist in me became depressed and the repressed feelings of the refugee took over. Will it ever end?

Before the trip, we had planned to surprise our daughters Michal and Suzie by celebrating their birthdays that afternoon. They were born within a few days of each other in late August. We all walked back to the hotel where, at the filmmakers' cue, we all walked into the room where Suzie and Michal were being interviewed. The surprise was complete, including the presents.

At the end of the dinner, to mark the momentous occasion of this family gathering, Menachem and I had decided to give each of the grandchildren a silver 'dog tag' on a neck chain inscribed as follows:

"Heidelberg/Hoffenheim September 4, 2005: The day I discovered my roots."

To see each of the grandchildren, ranging in age from two to twenty-two years old, come forward when called so that their grandfathers could hang the memento around their neck, was an unforgettable experience.

Our children had also made their own plans, and surprised us by presenting us, the grandfathers, with an album in which each of the children and grandchildren had written about their feelings and the significance of the family gathering; it was a very exciting moment.

Sunday, September 4, 2005. The charter bus departed from the hotel at 9 a.m. for a location 25 kilometers away. We were accompanied by Mr. Hartmut Riehl, the former school principal from Hoffenheim and a local historian.

Fred: We drove along the river and the railway line where so long ago, when I was eight years old, I had ridden on the same railway line back and forth to school after having been kicked out of the local elementary school for being Jewish. Those old suppressed feelings returned, remaining with me all that day – bitter and sweet, at the same time. The sweet – all of us together for once and likely never to be again. The bitter – having to relive everything all over again.

Menachem: We drove to Neidenstein – our mother's birthplace, which we once frequently walked to through the forests to visit grandmother. We walked through the village which was hillier than I remembered, and walked up the street locally known as Judenbuckel (Jews' humpback [what a name!]). We looked at the house our grandmother had lived in. We made no local contact, but Mr. Kurt Wuest, the local religious studies teacher, accompanied us. He is the one who, approximately two years ago, found and located for us the gravestones of our maternal grandfather and grandmother, in the Jewish cemetery of Waibstadt.

How appropriate then to move on to the regional Jewish cemetery of Waibstadt, five kilometers away. We entered the dark forest, climbed the hill brimming with memories, and found the grave markers of our grandparents, whom we never knew. We busied ourselves by removing weeds from the gravesites. In general, the cemetery was well maintained. Mr. Riehl explained that the local school made occasional trips to do some weeding. Because the inscription on some of the markers had been worn by time and weather, as noticed on a previous visit, Menachem brought with him metal plaques appropriately inscribed. David, Michal, Suzie, Jonathan and Zvi affixed these on the sandstone grave markers and Menachem recited the Kaddish, the prayer for the dead. It was a very moving scene.

We moved on to the eerily empty streets of Hoffenheim, looked at the spot where the synagogue had stood, the house across the street where we were born, 10 Kirchstrasse where we took refuge after Kristallnacht, the church, the post office steps where Menachem was bitten by a dog, the communal garden where our mother coaxed vegetables from the ground.

It's all there, neat, nothing out of place, except that there is no trace of a former Jewish community. Hitler had done a thorough job. But irony of irony, here we were, Menachem, Ingrid and I, bringing our descendants, all twenty-nine of them, to see from where they had hailed. There was no feeling of triumph, of having conquered the past. No, we felt more like strangers in an estranged land. Were it not for the Hopp family's warmth and care and that of the three pastors and their wives, it would have been unbearable.

The Meeting at the Community Hall and Unveiling of the Memorial Plaque

We drove back to Heidelberg to change clothes. At 3 p.m. we returned to Hoffenheim for the book launch and the unveiling of the memorial plaque to the deported. To our great surprise, in contrast to the morning walk in the village when we saw no one, the afternoon's affair in the community center was attended by close to 400 locals.

Following are the translated speeches.

Welcome by Mr. Hess

After the welcome and introductory notes by our mayor Herr Geinert I also want to welcome you on behalf of the village council and the people of Hoffenheim.

It is a great joy for us that you have come to participate as our guests in today's event, in Hoffenheim. Originally, this project was initiated by our former pastor, Wilfried Steiger, who unfortunately died some years ago; the project was then pursued by Pastors Ludwig Streib and Matthias Uhlig, as well as Hartmut Riehl, the president of our local history society and former head of our school Am großen Wald. Our special thanks go to the members of the Mayer family, the Raymes family, and the Hopp families, without whom today's event would not be possible.

Dear Mr. Mayer, dear Mr. Raymes, for the village of Hoffenheim, today, upon presentation of your book, is a day of particular significance, considering the background of those disastrous, dreadful and bitter events during the Hitler regime, which nowadays many people are unable to understand. Not that we could change anything! Today's event is significant simply because we have to join all our respective strengths and faculties to influence the present and the future in a way that similar catastrophes cannot happen again.

The contemporary witnesses of those atrocities are gradually dying out. Let us therefore always try to impart to our children and grandchildren, to all the young people, the fact that everyone is a foreigner – nearly everywhere. If we succeed in doing so, the ensuing tolerance and understanding for each other, as well as the interest in other countries and cultures, will prevent a repetition of such a holocaust.

Dear Mr. Mayer and family, dear Mr. Raymes and family. It is not only the presentation of the German edition of your book that has brought us together today, but also the fact that after so many years it has finally become possible to unveil a commemorative plaque with the names of all the Jewish citizens that were deported from Hoffenheim.

We are convinced that, with the plaque being affixed at the town hall, we have chosen the right place for it. We hope that these small steps toward reconciliation will be of the greatest significance for the future and peace among people. Let us further tolerance, understanding and consideration for others but firmly insist that they are practiced. Then we can, together, dream of peace among us and everybody in the world. In reference, I would like to quote a Brazilian bishop, "If one alone is dreaming, the dream is but a dream, but if two are dreaming, this is the beginning of a new reality!"

With these words in mind, I wish you all a pleasant time in harmony, as well as intensive and interesting conversations. We would be pleased if many of you would soon be our guests again in Hoffenheim.

The Dreadful End of the Jewish Community in the 20th Century – Pastor Ludwig Streib

As late as in the 20th century, the daily life of the Jews in Hoffenheim did not differ much, except in the religious aspect, from that of the Christians. Children between four and six years of age went to the Christian kindergarten, the older ones to the Volksschule (elementary school) or to the Gymnasium (high school) in Sinsheim. The adults worked in the village. Most of them were independent tradesmen and nearly all of them owned a house and a small piece of arable land. In 1933, sixteen houses belonged to Jewish citizens, twelve of them occupied by their owners. The Jews then were members in the local organizations and thought highly of by their neighbors.

But this normal course of life abruptly ended when the Nazis came to power. All at once, laws discriminating Jews were enacted. First, Christians were forbidden to buy in Jewish shops, an enormous problem as in Hoffenheim nearly all Jews were tradesmen. Christians who kept buying from them were denounced as being Judenknechte (Jew knaves) and announced as such on a notice board where the rabble-rousing paper *Der Sturmer* was displayed. Later on, Jews were no longer allowed to work for Christians. (My grandfather's name, for instance, was put up on the notice board because he let Helmut Mayer – your first cousin, Aunt Elsa's son, who was murdered in Auschwitz at age twenty-three – work with him in his field.)

The decrees became more and more drastic. Jews were no longer allowed to shop during regular opening hours of German-owned shops, and non-Jewish citizens were forbidden to mix with Jews. Jews had to add the first name Sarah and Israel to their names.

As a result of these discriminations some families emigrated, which was by no means a simple affair. The voyage was expensive and in some countries you needed a person who stood surety for you. Additionally, they were Hoffenheimers, and that was the greater problem: this is where they were born and had grown up, where their forefathers were buried, and this is where they were at home. Why should they leave? That's why, for instance, Heinrich Friedmann waited until 1940 to emigrate. He then had to flee via Russia and Japan to get to the United States of America. Only twenty-one out of fifty-three Jews who still lived in Hoffenheim emigrated.

1938 was a year that brought a drastic and decisive break in the life of the remaining Jews. During the night of November 9th, later called Kristallnacht, the synagogues were set ablaze all over Germany. In Hoffenheim, the local storm troopers led the action during which the synagogue was demolished; the beams and the inventory were taken to the fields outside Hoffenheim near the road to Sinsheim and set alight, going up in flames.

The Mayer family, who had been living in an apartment adjacent to the synagogue, had to take refuge in the house of their relatives. All Jewish men were arrested and taken to the Dachau concentration camp for at least four weeks. When they returned, they had to perform forced labor, and among other things they had to build the *Obere Schießmauerstraße*.

On October 22, 1940, the terror culminated. The eighteen Jews who were still living in the village, seven women, seven men and four children, had to pack their suitcases within a few hours. Each person was only allowed to take along fifty kilograms of luggage and 100 Reichsmark. They had to assemble in the town hall from where they were taken away by truck. They were then taken by train to the detention camp in Gurs in the south of France, and to Rivesaltes. The living conditions there were inhuman. Then, in 1942, they were transported back to Germany and onwards to Poland, to be murdered in Auschwitz.

Only the four children, who were rescued by various welfare organizations, survived. The fourteen adults all died a dreadful death. And what was the people of Hoffenheim's reaction to this? Their reactions varied. The Nazis had ordered that the inventory of the deported people's houses be registered. This was done rather superficially and some property was stolen. Only when others published a poem naming the culprits, was most of the stolen property returned. The reactions varied also in other respects.

Some people were quite enthusiastic when it came to discriminating against and tormenting Jews, others were full of consternation about it and felt ashamed, continued to be friendly and supported them secretly with food, and wept when they were deported. But nobody dared revolt against these actions because they were afraid.

Thus the history of the Jewish community of Hoffenheim came to an end on October 22, 1940, and the majority of its members had to endure a frightful death in Auschwitz in August 1942.

The History of the Memorial Plaque – Pastor Mathias Uhlig

Forty years after the Kristallnacht, in November 1978, the youth organization of the Protestant church of Hoffenheim discussed the history of Jewish life in Hoffenheim and the fact that Kristallnacht activities had also taken place in their own village. In March 1979, Pastor Wilfried Steiger and this group applied to the local Hoffenheim authorities to install a commemorative plaque at the place where the synagogue had once stood. Since the village council didn't find a suitable location nearby, it was decided to affix it to the belfry wall next to the cemetery chapel.

In 1984, a commemorative plaque for the dead soldiers of World War II was affixed next to the Memorial to the Dead of the 1870-71 war and World War I. As a result of this rearrangement of the memorials, the plaque at the belfry was removed and affixed to the cemetery wall.

At a parish conference in the summer of 1987, school dean Lohrbacher told me about the brothers Fred Raymes and Menachem Mayer, and let me have the address of the latter who was then staying in Paris. Until then, in the Protestant parish, no former Jewish Hoffenheimer was known to have uttered the wish to contact the inhabitants of his birthplace. I personally set great store in such a contact and therefore traveled to Paris and visited Menachem and his family. It was amazing that Menachem then let me have the originals of nearly all the letters his parents had written in the concentration camps. I am sure he didn't have any copies, and if so, they must have been in poor condition. The confidence he thus placed in me was very moving.

In 1989, Ludwig Streib conducted research on the history of the Jewish community in Hoffenheim and wrote a thesis on the subject. Thanks to this work we have personal reports by inhabitants of Hoffenheim about their experiences until 1940.

Between 1989 and 1994, close to 120 citizens of Hoffenheim and their friends visited Israel and while there also met Menachem. One specific day in Jerusalem left a deep impression on me, when Gisela Heinlein, on the terrace of Menachem's house, presented him with a drawing of the Hoffenheim synagogue, which Werner Rudisile had drawn from memory. I was very pleased to see it again when visiting Menachem this year.

In 1995, I moved to Achern and the ties between Jerusalem and me weakened. When I left Hoffenheim, Werner Rudisile gave me the bankbook with the donation for the planned book to remind me "not to forget what you planned." Well, it was not forgotten, but postponed as other things prevailed. What a surprise, when three years ago Menachem sent us the English translation of his book. He had undertaken the very job I had planned on accomplishing. Now there were no more excuses for not acting, and so the English edition of the book was sent to several friends in Hoffenheim who were asked to contribute financial support.

It was a great help that the Hopp siblings spontaneously promised to further the project when they were informed of its existence by Pastor Bar and the Berberig family. They proved to be very proactive and in gaining significant financial assistance.

Innumerable letters, faxes and e-mails were exchanged every week, sometimes daily, between Dossenheim, Achern, Jerusalem and Florida. The fact that the joint efforts we undertook have developed into a feeling of friendship shows everybody's great concern and empathy.

Between January and May 2004, Frau Franke completed the German translation. Her experience was particularly necessary when some original German quotations had to be retraced and the original German wording of the parents' letters had to be reinserted into the excerpts of the English version. Thereafter, it took Ludwig Streib and myself longer than we had originally expected to complete the project, trying to pay more attention to some details. The present version of the book was completed together with Jochen Baumgartner and Theresa Sittig.

Today I can say that in view of all our activities leading to today's gathering I somehow have the feeling that God has heard our prayers. When I started studying theology in 1972, one of the theories in German universities was that God was dead. One of my professors asked, "How can you believe in God after Auschwitz?" I have never believed in this sort of theology but I have given it a lot of thought. Today I would answer the question as follows, "After Auschwitz, Christians can believe in God only together with Jews."

The Responsibility of Today's Generation – Dr. Ruediger Hopp

Today we have assembled to inaugurate a plaque commemorating the eighteen Jewish citizens who were deported from Hoffenheim during the Third Reich.

Fourteen of them were murdered in Auschwitz, four of them, children, were deported to France and survived the war. They survived the nightmare of the Nazi tyranny in an odyssey leading them through a great number of orphanages and hiding places. Today we can welcome three of them, as well as the members of their families who accompanied them to Hoffenheim.

It is impossible to imagine the suffering and horror these four went through, as did their murdered parents and relatives. We bow to their grief. But those who survived have not turned away from us in hatred and bitterness but have come here to see how we are dealing with our infamous historical heritage. The fact that we are inaugurating this commemorative plaque only 65 years after the deportation is truly nothing we can be proud of. But the fact that we are doing it elicits hope. Hope for a responsible way of dealing with our history and the lessons that have to be learned from it. For, if I may quote from the book that is being presented to the public today, "Those who ignore history are bound to relive it."

During the twelve years of Hitler's regime, the most atrocious crimes known in history were committed in the name of our people. We, the generations born after this time, are not guilty of, or responsible for these crimes. But we have to accept this heritage as we have accepted the positive legacies of our people. We are deeply ashamed of the crimes committed by Germans but we do not have to be ashamed of being German. If the act of remembrance of the Holocaust is to make sense, it must have the aim of preventing a relapse into a similar political barbarity. This is definitely a task facing us, for time and again the peoples of the world are tempted to fall prey to totalitarian systems.

Unfortunately, history and the present times teach us that if there is a choice between good and evil, people tend to be more attracted by evil than good. If everything is permitted, and if people are even publicly honored for evil deeds, many even enjoy committing such deeds. The varnish of civilization is easily destroyed and it is practically a miracle that good exists.

Our task now, yours and ours, is to defend good from evil. The Jewish community rightly claims that the history of their sufferings should not be forgotten and that the Germans should adopt a responsible way of dealing with the "heritage of guilt."

I would like to add to our request that you give us, who want to accept this responsibility, the opportunity to participate in a worldwide alliance furthering good and suppressing evil in the world. Together we will have to transform the traumatic events of the past into hope for the future.

Inauguration of the memorial plaque in Hoffenheim – Menachem

Close to 65 years ago, we stood here: my brother Manfred/ Fred, eleven years old at the time; my cousin, Inge/Ingrid, four, and myself, eight years old, just like our grandchildren Roni, Rotem, Briana and Shachar who are here today standing close to me.

On the morning of October 22, 1940, together with our parents and all the other Jewish citizens, we were driven out of our homes, pushed on a truck and together with 6,500 Jews of Baden and the Palatinate deported to the Gurs detention camp, in the south of France.

Eight months later, on June 4, 1941, our mother wrote to us, her children, who succeeded to get out of the camp and were living in hiding, "Spring has passed. How times flies – what will become of us? I miss the forest. Do you remember our walks in the forest, two to four hours walking to Neidenstein? When the beautiful castle came into view, we recited the poem Welcome to the Sunshine. Do you remember when we went to Steinsfurt?..."

Fourteen months later she couldn't welcome the sunshine, as she was devoured by the hell of Auschwitz. In August 1942, we received our parents' last letter:

Rivesaltes, 10th August, 1942
My dear children,
I want to write a few lines quickly before the journey. Seeing that we are leaving and we are only permitted to take one piece of hand luggage, I sent you the chest of clothes yesterday evening. If you

go to America, take with you whatever is necessary. With the help of God, perhaps we will also get there. Give our regards to Aunt Elsa when you write to her. I don't know whether we'll be able to write to you – perhaps through the Red Cross. Be good children.

Your Mother, who loves you

My dear children,

Just a few lines before we leave – I don't know where we're going. We don't in the least regret leaving you behind, you are safer where you are. Perhaps you will hear everything.

Be well. All the best and kisses from your Mother. Dear Manfred and Heinz, be good to one another – that's my greatest concern.

Our parents at that time were in the same age group as our children, present here: Jonathan, Suzie, Michal, David, Renee and Zvi.

How were those awful events possible in the civilized, rational, scientific, cultured, and enlightened Germany and the world of the twentieth century?

The Israeli poet Zelda (1914-1984), reminds us in her poem that each person lost in the Holocaust was a unique individual and that every prisoner with a number tattooed on his or her arm in the concentration camp had a name.

Unto Every Person There is a Name

Unto every person there is a name
Bestowed upon him by God
And given him by his father and mother

Unto every person there is a name
Accorded him by his stature
And the manner of his smile
And given him by his style of dress

Unto every person there is a name
Conferred on him by the mountains
And given him by his neighbors

Unto every person there is a name
Assigned him by his sins
And given him by his yearnings

Unto every person there is a name
Given him by his enemies
And given him by his love

Unto every person there is a name
Derived from his festivals
And given him by his labor

Unto every person there is a name
Presented him by the seasons
And given him by his blindness

Unto every person there is a name
Bestowed on him by the sea
And given him by his death.

Today, with the inauguration of this memorial plaque and the publication of our book in German, our parents and the other murdered Jewish citizens of Hoffenheim are wrested once more from oblivion. By these events here, in this small village of Hoffenheim, the facts and reality of the Holocaust are transmitted once more to the entire post-Holocaust generation.

It is said that one must learn from history and differentiate between victims and perpetrators, actions and results, causes and effects, guilt and responsibility.

I would like to thank, also on behalf of Ingrid and Fred, especially Mrs. Karola Muehlburger and brothers Dr. Ruediger and Dietmar Hopp, who took the initiative to establish this memorial plaque and who made the publication of the German edition of our book possible.

Many thanks also to the Pastors Matthias Uhlig and Ludwig Streib and to Mr. Hartmut Riehl, Chairman of the Heimatsverein in Hoffenheim, who were involved in the book's publication. Thanks to their efforts, it reached fruition.

We consider all of you – you who embraced the obligation to remember these past horrendous events – as innocent members of Germany's contemporary generation.

Fifteen to twenty years ago, Pastor Uhlig asked me whether I was ready to bridge the distance between Jerusalem and Hoffenheim. At that time, my answer was 'no', explaining that a bridge needs to be supported at both ends, while it seems to me that this bridge had only one pillar at that time, namely Jerusalem. Our parents and the other murdered Jewish citizens of Hoffenheim didn't empower me to raise the missing pillar.

Today, we are ready and are able to outstretch our hands to people with goodwill, who are ready to remember that "remembrance is the secret redemption".

I Speak on Behalf of the Second Generation – Michal

> *I was not among the six million who perished in the Holocaust.*
> *I was not among them, but the fire and the smoke remain with me.*
> *The pillars of fire and pillars of smoke show me*
> *the way, night and day. And the frenzied search remains with me...*
> Yehuda Amichai, Israeli poet

To be part of the second generation means to spend one's entire life following the pillars of fire and smoke. To live constantly with the frenzied search, even though one does not always know what one seeks.

For every one of us, this search is an indivisible part of our personal identity. It means growing up in the shadow of stories that were never told. It means that as we reach maturity, we begin to ask questions for which there are no answers. It means that we are extremely curious about the letters that are hidden in the drawer. We constantly pester our father to translate them.

As we stand today in Hoffenheim we are seeking part of ourselves. We are living the story of two children. It is almost like sitting on our grandparents' knees and hearing about their lives and their past – something which, to our great sorrow, has been denied us. We miss it very much.

We close our eyes and look, there's our grandmother, a young woman walking in the woods with her two small children. She tells them stories and sings songs. She waits for them at the train station when they come home from school. In our imagination we can see our father and Fred playing here, in the yard. Horrified, we watch grandfather being taken to the labor camp. We see the synagogue in flames. Kristallnacht. The family is driven out and broken up.

We try but we cannot understand the feelings and emotions of the parents, forever separated from their children. What would have happened but for…? To be here now means to transform virtual memory into reality, to know that we didn't come from nowhere – we come from somewhere, and we take great pride in our roots. We owe a great deal to our parents. They provided us with normal, happy lives, despite the memories. This is not something we take for granted. We are very grateful to our father and Fred for the opportunity to return to our roots and to the past.

Despite great emotional hardship they dared to write this fascinating story for us and for future generations. This was a noble and great deed for us and for future generations. Not many people are capable of doing so. I hope and believe that you found an element of healing in the writing. We – the next generations – have a great obligation towards our parents and grandparents, towards our children and their children. It is our duty to preserve this memory. Moreover, we are required to learn from it. The lessons are clear – we must work towards a better world, free of hate and injustice.

We are grateful to the Hopp siblings who made this event possible. They are living proof that there are good people in the world who stretch out their hands in peace and atonement.

Today we have a rare opportunity to come full circle. Here, in the place where our family arose, in the place where they were torn apart by killing and hatred, in this very place, our family comes together once again in the spirit of life, without hate, without racism, and with the desire for reconciliation and peace.

May He who makes peace on high bring peace upon us and on all Israel. And let us say, Amen.

Unveiling the Memorial Plaque

From the community center we walked to the City Hall, the very place from which we were deported, now the site of the memorial plaque, which we had come to unveil.

One by one an adult, accompanied by a grandchild, the descendants of the murdered, lit candles and called out the name of the family member. This was repeated 14 times. Menachem repeated the Kaddish, a prayer that surely has not been heard in Hoffenheim for the past 65 years.

The plaque, affixed at the very spot of deportation, reads:

> *From this location on 22 October 1940, eighteen Jewish citizens were deported from Hoffenheim. Followed by the names.*
> *May this plaque remind us of the suffering of the murdered and deported. Always and above all it should warn and oblige us to behave with humanity and tolerance.*

After signing close to 150 books on the street, which had been closed to traffic, local people had the opportunity to talk to us. Some of them said, "Our families were neighbors, don't you remember?" One strange and weird story in particular stands out.

The memorial plaque

Menachem: One woman, in her fifties, approached me and to my astonishment asked me, as she was crying: "Are you ready to take something from me?"

I said, "What are you talking about?" She said, "I am Ms. W. In my home, which I inherited from my parents, is a cabinet. One of the drawers contains a fork, which no one wants to, or is allowed to, touch, as if it were cursed!"

She continued, "My family lived near your house; when in November 1938 you were driven out of your home (Kristallnacht), my mother told me that the fork was stolen from your family's belongings. I would like to return it to the rightful owners. Are you ready to accept it from me? I said, "Of course."

A few weeks later, I received a small parcel with the cutlery and an attached letter. Ms. W. wrote:

Dear Dr. Mayer,
When I opened the drawer, I also found a spoon and a knife with the same pattern. Somehow I remembered only a fork. As I told

you they were never used, since it was known that they wrongfully became part of our belongings. I am glad that I can hand over the cutlery to you and thank you for accepting it...

Yours,
E. W.

This took place 65 years later. One of only two physical objects from our parents. The pocket watch and now the cutlery for a single setting.

We reboarded the bus for dinner at the St. Leo-Rot Country Club at the invitation of Dietmar Hopp. After cocktails on the lawn and a photograph session, dinner was served.

Dietmar Hopp extended his welcome and expressed his gratitude that they were able to make the day's events successful. This was followed by a thank-you speech by Fred to the entire Hopp family for making these unforgettable events possible.

Fred: Words fail me to describe the momentous events that all of us have experienced over the past several days. I would like to begin my comments with the ending statement to make sure that I don't forget them in all the excitement.

The fork, spoon and knife

Sitting on the lawn: Hadass Mayer, Ilana Mayer, Yuval Tur-Paz Shachar Mayer, Rotem Mayer, Roni Tur-Paz, Cameron Raymes, Connor Raymes
Seated on the chairs: Dietmar Hopp, Fred Raymes, Karola Muehlburger, Menachem Mayer with Nizan, Ruediger Hopp
Third row: Zvi Mayer with Lior, Michal Tur-Paz, Ayala Mayer, Ingrid Sachs, Lydia Raymes, Chava Mayer, Katie Herr, Suzie Biagi, Eric Biagi, Briana Raymes, Charles Sachs
Fourth row: Omer Tur-Paz, Renee Sachs-Day, Jonathan Mayer, Livnat Mayer, Merav Mayer, David Raymes, Joyce Raymes, Tal Tur-Paz

How do we express our thanks to the Hopp family for bringing us all together for this once-in-a-lifetime event? How do we salute them for having the courage to reopen feelings long dormant so that they may better heal? How do we thank Mrs. Karola Muehlburger and Dr. Ruediger Hopp for proposing and sponsoring the memorial plaque to the deported, dedicated this afternoon? How do we thank them for making the publication of our book in German possible? How do we thank Dr. Ruediger Hopp for spending endless hours arranging all the details for this event: the travel, hotel, bus and tour arrangements, airport pickup, and yes, even kosher food? A Herculean effort.

And last but not least how do we thank Mr. Dietmar Hopp who enabled this extraordinary gathering? How did it come about that an eleven-year-old, forever separated from his parents, who for years rejected all that was German, suppressed his mother tongue, denied his Jewishness, and refused to buy neither a VW nor a Braun razor, how is it possible that sixty years later he can sit at this table and break bread with you?

Let me tell you that this acceptance has taken years. The first time I returned to Germany was thirty-two years after the deportation. As soon as the plane landed in Frankfurt I made a dash for Hoffenheim, drawn to it like a magnet to iron. I walked the village and woods but was afraid to make contact with anyone. I felt depressed, abandoned, and alone. Why had I come? What was I looking for? I was a stranger in an estranged land.

It took another twenty years to return for the second time, which I did in 1992 with my brother Menachem, after having visited that hell on earth, Auschwitz. We decided to come to Hoffenheim once more as a shared experience. Pastor Uhlig had invited us and arranged for a few Hoffenheimers to be present in the church's backyard. The very church whose bells I mentioned in the book because I so loved their sound. One notable Hoffenheimer in the group was a young Seminary student, Ludwig Streib, who had written a thesis entitled, *The Jewish Community of Hoffenheim*. He asked about our family history, which he wanted to clarify, but I had few answers for him.

With this encounter I came to realize there were Germans who possessed goodwill, who cared deeply about the past and were searching for ways to make amends. Incidentally, Pastor Streib did such a thorough job in researching his thesis that he unearthed my fifty-six year old first grade report card from the Hoffenheimer elementary school – I have never forgiven him for that.

The third time I made social contact with a German was in a parking lot of a restaurant in Sarasota, Florida, just eight months ago. My wife Lydia and I had agreed to meet Dr. Ruediger Hopp and his sister Karola for lunch. We had never seen each other. But on recognition, Ruediger stepped towards me with an outstretched hand and uttered these unforgettable words, "Thank you Mr. Raymes for being willing to shake our hands."

Willing! Can you imagine the meaning of the word "willing"?
The emotions were overwhelming; we embraced and I knew from
that moment on that we had met someone who has also suffered
over the years. The rest is history in the making.

Two Months Later

Two months after the meeting we returned to Hoffenheim – this
time, to film a documentary. Menachem kept a diary during the
period of filming: November 6-17, 2005.

Sunday, November 6, 2005

Menachem: We landed at Frankfurt Airport at midday and
immediately began filming. This is my sixth visit to Hoffenheim.
How strange. For many years I was convinced I would never go
back. I didn't want to return to the place that threw out my family
and myself. But on the other hand, I was also drawn to the place
of my lost childhood as if by the enchanted music played by the
Piper of Hamelin.

Monday, November 7, 2005

The night passed uneventfully, I was even able to sleep. Fred is
expected to arrive from the United States this afternoon. This
morning Ruediger Hopp came to the hotel to take me to various
places in Hoffenheim. Ruediger is making a sincere effort to
interest me in these places of my origin, but to his great regret
he is unsuccessful. Something within me is dead. The sights are
astonishingly beautiful, clean and aesthetic, but they don't ignite a
spark in me. The places where I played as a child do not arouse in me
a sense of belonging. Ruediger and I continued to stroll the lanes of
Hoffenheim, recalling the memories they evoked: the shoemaker,

the barbershop, storks nesting on red roofs, the train station, the houses where our families lived. He also revealed intimate details about his parents' home, telling me about his father, mother and siblings, and events within his family. Fred arrived in the afternoon and immediately (how typical of him!) we set out to walk from our hotel in the village of Zusenhausen to Hoffenheim. The distance between the two villages is no more than three or four kilometers and the road winds between fields, through the enchanted forest and the river. How often we walked this way with Mother.

Tuesday, November 8, 2005

We spent the entire day filming.

We travel through fields where young men are harvesting sugar beets, and the forests surrounding Hoffenheim. The large car holds the driver, Ofra the director, Ronit the editor, Klaus the cameraman and the assistant in charge of the sound system, and of course Fred and myself. It's a bit crowded. They film during the journey. I remembered how Hoffenheim looked when I was a child, from the inside; in other words, looking out from inside my house. Now the perspective is different – a general, comprehensive picture, from the outside in. Yellow colza flowers gild the fertile green fields, the trees are shedding their leaves. The village of Hoffenheim peeps through the morning mist, and I keep asking myself, "Why? Why? What is the connection between aesthetic beauty and evil, between satiety and wickedness?" As the prophet Jeremiah asks, "Why does the path of the wicked flourish?" The eternal question of why the righteous suffer while the wicked prosper gives me no rest.

During the journey Ofra asks, "What do you feel toward your birthplace?"

Fred: I have no positive feelings for this place. To tell you the truth, I don't feel a sense of connectedness to any place at all. Even my feeling of belonging to the United States is not absolute.

Menachem: I don't feel any connection to this place. I'm curious to recognize, to know and understand. My homeland is Israel. That's how I felt from the first moment I arrived, I dare say even before that. On the ship bringing me to Israel I ripped up all the papers and documents in my possession. I was symbolically leaving the past behind and opening a new chapter. Homeland means belonging, identity, history, mutual involvement, shared destiny – none of these things is in Hoffenheim, the place of my birth.

In the afternoon we arrived in Neuestrasse, where the synagogue and our house had stood until they were destroyed 67 years ago, on the morning of November 10, 1938, the day known as Kristallnacht. The film producers had arranged for us to meet with a non-Jewish childhood friend, bringing him from the other side of Germany for the occasion. The Gehrig family had lived next door to us. They had many children and were very poor. The tenth child, Paul, was my age, and we spent a great deal of time together.

The meeting was very emotional, especially for Paul. Something inside me died a long time ago. Paul recalled childhood memories from when we were between three and six years old. It's amazing how many little, commonplace stories evoked strong feelings in me, stories about small events that Paul remembered, although I didn't. I was astonished by every detail. Paul described our mother washing clothes on a washboard in the yard in front of our house, adding matter-of-factly that "we didn't even have a washboard." After she finished, my mother would pour out the water from the tub into the open ditch carrying water to the sewer drain at the side of the road. He told me that we, Paul and I, waited for this moment so we could sail paper boats in the flowing water. I'm learning new things about myself – I was a child and I played with my friend next door!

Paul went on to say that on Christmas Eve my mother brought them a box of old toys and clothes. "We thought you were rich," he said, and added, "I clearly remember what your mother looked like." Why does he remember, when I can't?

Paul related how a group of Hitler-Jugend (members of the Hitler youth organization) came to the synagogue during the festival prayer services. They flung open the door, blew a blast on a trumpet and fled. This is how Paul described the morning of the pogrom on November 10, 1938:

In the morning Emile Hopp appeared at the head of a group of five or six SA men (Nazi storm-troopers), all carrying hoes or pickaxes. They went into your house and the synagogue and started smashing everything. In the afternoon, another, larger, group of SA men arrived from the nearby village of Zuzenhausen and joined in the destruction. They threw things out through the second floor windows of your house: furniture, clothes, and cooking utensils. Some things landed on the dung heap in our yard. For years I kept two of your belongings: one was a blue porcelain box with a lid, shaped like a dove. The other was a book of stories about Moses in the bulrushes, Moses and the burning bush, and the Children of Israel crossing the Red Sea. The book was colorful, with gilded illustrations. It was my first book, that's how I learned to read. I left home and don't know what happened to the two items. I left Hoffenheim a long time ago, I never liked the atmosphere there.

While we were standing in the square where the synagogue once stood, curious neighbors began to take notice, attracted by the hustle and bustle of the film crew. Several peered through their windows, and one man sneaked a peek from around the corner of the opposite house, 11 Neuestrasse, the house where Fred and I were born. When he saw me looking at him he swiftly vanished. I went after him and found him waiting for me. I said, "I am Jewish. I was born here. Perhaps you can tell me something about my family, about the synagogue, or about the Jews here?" His reply was typical, "I don't know anything. I wasn't born here." "Surely your parents told you something," I asked. He replied, "I know nothing."

At this point his wife emerged from the house, yelling, "Leave us alone. Stop digging up the past. We also had it bad, we were bombed by American planes…"

I asked, "How can you compare intentional, government-planned genocide to bombs in wartime?" "Get out, you won't find anything here!" She continued to shout, an evil smile plastered on her face.

A woman of about my age came out of 4 Neuestrasse. She told us that her parents and ours were close friends, adding that she had a cabinet that our parents gave her family. I was very excited and asked to see it. The woman invited us into her home and we followed her. In one of the second floor rooms stood a handsome cabinet made of red cherry wood, with four drawers below and two glass doors above. It was the first time I had ever seen something from home! I asked her why my mother gave it to her parents and she replied that her parents used to light "the fire and the light" in my parents' house.

Another piece of the puzzle – what a welter of emotions! My childhood friend, my mother doing the laundry, Heinz – little Menachem – floating paper boats, an illustrated book, and now a real, three-dimensional object! I told myself that I had to buy the cabinet and bring it home, and told Ruediger Hopp of my decision. "Leave it to me," he said, "I'll take care of it." So far Ruediger hasn't managed to fulfill his promise. Meanwhile I have a photograph of the cabinet.

The cabinet

Wednesday, November 9, 2005

This morning they're filming us on the train from Hoffenheim to Heidelberg. For two years we took the train to attend the Jewish school in Heidelberg: starting from Kristallnacht, November 10, 1938, the day we were expelled from the local school because Jewish children were no longer permitted to study with Aryan children, until October 21, 1940, the day we were sent to the camp in France.

They keep filming inside the carriage. This ought to attract the attention of the other passengers, but they behave in typical German fashion: everyone sits there, gazing into space, looking away as if nothing was happening. "We saw nothing, we know nothing."

We returned to Hoffenheim, this time for a discussion with our friends, the three pastors: Albrecht Lohrbacher, Matthias Uhlig, and Ludwig Streib.

The question posed to them was what prompted each of them to forge ties with Judaism in general and with the State of Israel in particular. Each one gave his own reasons in his own words.

The pastors. Left to right: Fred, Pastors Uhlig, Streib, and Lohrbacher, Menachem

Uhlig stressed the theological aspect, referring to the holy book he was holding (the Bible). "Nine-tenths of the Holy Writings are common to both Christians and Jews. The New Testament belongs only to us, the Christians, and it only comprises one-tenth of the book."

It appeared to me that Streib placed more emphasis on the sociological aspect. He related to the fact that human rights, which were an integral part of German society, were denied to Jews. In this connection he said his grandfather told him that in the village, our father was nicknamed *Kappenfresser* (hat-eater). The name stuck to him after Father said, "If I'm wrong, I'll eat my hat."

Lohrbacher demonstrated an unconditional love for Israel. He said, "A few days ago my wife and I returned from one of our visits to Israel. We felt very good. We met with interesting people. We feel much better in Israel than we do in Germany, and were it not for the fact that we have children here, we would seriously consider living in Israel." Later that day we went for a walk in the forest, that same forest where we walked with Mother and Father on our way to visit Grandmother Mina in Neidenstein. The trees

In the forest

are shedding their leaves. The forest evokes memories of its mossy smell, its vivid colors, the call of the cuckoo, fearful German folk stories about the wicked witch living in the depths of the forest, the wolf and Little Red Riding Hood. Is it merely a coincidence that these dark tales originated right here, on German soil?

I think this will be my last visit to Hoffenheim. But that's what I said after each of my previous five visits. What will be? Only time will tell.

France: Sunday, November 13, 2005

On the previous Friday, we arrived at the hotel in Pau. It is actually an ancient castle renovated to function as a modern hotel. From here we will set out to film various sites, returning every evening.

Yesterday was Shabbat and we took a break from filming. Fred and I went for a walk along the promenade, with its breathtaking view of the snow-covered Pyrenees. A similar view could be seen from the Gurs detention camp, but who ever looked?

A colorful parade was taking place in the square outside the Pau town hall, attended by French army veterans. The ceremony commemorated victims of the First and Second World Wars, the heroism of the soldiers, and the exploits of freedom fighters during World War II. The speeches were living proof of how history is engendered in the collective memory. It appeared from the speeches that the French were all righteous, they all opposed the Nazis, and all fought in the Resistance, liberating their country from the Germans. And I ask, "Where were the people who collaborated with the Germans, the guards in the camps, the engine drivers whose trains transported the victims to the extermination camps?"

Today we traveled to Gurs. Its appearance reflects the French attitude towards historical memory: apart from the narrow road that bisected the camp in our time, and the rotting wooden signs carved with single letters (A, B, etc.), there's nothing to be seen. Many trees have been planted on both sides of the road, the forest covers everything – the horror and the memory. An innocent passer-by can have no idea of what went on here. It is part and parcel of the policy of denial that says, "whatever doesn't exist, never existed."

We located the grave of Grandmother Mina in the cemetery on the outskirts of the camp. She was spared transportation to the gas chambers of Auschwitz.

Ofra presses me to recall facts and feelings from those days. I can't make her understand that I am unable and probably also unwilling to feel what I felt at the time. When it was all taking place we were simply preoccupied with staying alive. I feel for the survivors who have not been able to forget and to rid themselves of their experiences. I have forgotten many events. I can reconstruct many facts, both from personal memory and from documents – but I cannot evoke and recall the atmosphere of the time. Forgetfulness is a blessing.

In the afternoon we visited Jacqueline, the nursemaid at Aspet who served as my mother-figure. She was 18 at the time; today she is 84. For the past six months she has been in a convalescent retirement home. She was happy to see me but didn't recognize Fred. She looks good and well cared for. Her younger sister Mimi looks after her. Jacqueline's memory is not reliable. Her short-term memory is good but her recall of the past is vague and indistinct. It is sad to see her like this, but she seems happy. Forgetfulness is a blessing.

Tuesday, November 15, 2005

The village of Aspet nestles in a small valley surrounded by wooded mountains. Not far off, snow-capped mountain peaks can be seen. The orphanage is on the outskirts of the sleepy village. Today it functions as an institution for children with special educational needs. The principal and his staff welcomed us, some of them visibly moved at the sight of two veteran "graduates". Our arrival with the film crew disrupted their daily routine, attracting a great deal of attention and excitement. The teacher, a charming young woman in her twenties, prepared the children for our arrival.

The main building had been the center of our world from 1941 to 1943. It still looks exactly as it did 63 years ago. The old dormitories have been divided into small, homely rooms.

We wandered around, recalling bittersweet memories from those innocent years: playing in the yard; Jacqueline and Nelly, our nurse and social worker; slaughtering a calf with a pick-axe (one of the locals told us that it was the routine method of slaughtering beasts); the incessant hunger, beatings and punishments; hikes; stealing sweet forbidden fruit; hoarding bread under our mattresses for our planned visit with our parents; waiting for letters from our parents, which stopped arriving towards the end, when we had no way of knowing that they were no longer alive.

One of the children asked K., the German cameraman, "Where are you from?"

"I'm from Germany," he replied. That week the eleven year old had been learning about world wars, and he also knew we were coming, so his next question was, "Why did you kill the Jews?" Annoyed, the photographer replied, "Those were Nazis, not Germans!!!" K. is upset that we're focusing on German wickedness. But what else can we do? It is the scarlet thread that winds its way all through the documentary film.

Auschwitz-Birkenau: Thursday, November 17, 2005

I often ponder the eternal question of why the righteous suffer and the wicked prosper, or, as Jeremiah asks, "Why does the path of the wicked flourish?"

We passed through the gate where freight trains entered on their way to the ramp. Standing on the track I seemed to hear the sound of an approaching train. How symbolic – it was cold, wet and snowing. A flock of black ravens wheeled overhead, cawing as they came to roost on the gate adorned with the slogan "*Arbeit*

Macht Frei" (Work Makes You Free). Had I believed, I would have said they were the reincarnation of the storm troopers.

I ask myself, "What was the engine driver thinking as he bit into his sausage sandwich? What did he feel when he stopped the train alongside the ramp?"

Many ask, "Where was God?"

Some people lost their faith, arriving at the logical conclusion that after Auschwitz there is no God. For others, God is the "alibi" – this was God's will, so it is neither their responsibility nor their problem.

I am frequently asked how I handle the theological question. I don't know how God conducts His world. I don't understand Him. I despise those who pretend to know God's intentions, appointing themselves His accountants. Even Moses the Lawgiver, who sought to see God, was told, "no man can see Me, and live."[83]

How easy it is to absolve oneself of responsibility, placing it instead on God! The people in Auschwitz were all human beings: both the victims and those who perpetrated the crime. Mankind has freedom of choice. They and they alone are responsible for their actions. My God wasn't in Auschwitz, so when I come here, I am able to recite Kaddish.

---

83 Exodus 33:20

Bibliography

Arad, Yitzchak, Gutman, Israel, Margoliot, David, eds., *Documents on the Holocaust: Selected Sources on the Destruction of the Jews in Germany, Austria, Poland, and the Soviet Union*, Jerusalem 1987.

Beisel, Peter, *Die Geschichte der Juden in unsere Region*, Neidenstein 1989.

Blumenthal, W. Michael, *The Invisible Wall – Germans and Jews, A Personal Exploration*, Washington 1998.

Cornwell, John, *Hitler's Pope: The Secret History of Pius XII*, New York 2000.

Dawidowicz, Lucy S., *The War Against the Jews 1933–1945*, New York 1975, 1976.

Gilbert, Martin, *The Holocaust: The History of the Jews of Europe during the Second World War*, New York 1987.

Gobittz, Gerard, *Les Deportations de Refugies de Zone Libre en 1942*, Paris 1996.

Goldhagen, Daniel Jonah, *Hitler's Willing Executioners: Ordinary Germans and the Holocaust*, New York 1996.

Grynberg, Anne, *Les Camps de la Honte – les Internes Juifs dans les Camps Franpais*, Paris 1991.

Gutman, Israel, ed. *Encyclopedia of the Holocaust*, New York 1990.

Hahn, Joachim, *Errinerungen und Zeugnisse – Judische Geschichte in Baden-Würtemberg*, Stuttgart 1988.

Heymann, Raymond, "Hommage a Andree Salomon," in *Editions des Temoinages*, Jerusalem 1986.

Hundsnuscher, Franz and Taddy, Gerhard, *Die Jüdischen Gemeinden in Baden*, Stuttgart 1968.

Israelitisches Gemeindeblatt (Baden), 1922-1938.

Klarsfeld, Serge, *Le Memorial de la Deportation des Juifs de France*, Paris 1978.

Laharie, Claude, *Le Camp de Gurs, 1939-1945*, 1985.

Lazare, Lucien, *Rescue as Resistance: How Jewish Organizations Fought the Holocaust in France*, New York 1996.

LeBor, Adam, *Hitler's Secret Bankers: The Myth of Swiss Neutrality during the Holocaust*, Secaucus N.J. 1997.

Levy, Claude, *La Grande Rafle du Vel d'Hiv*, Paris 1967.

Marrus, Michael Robert, *Vichy France and the Jews*, New York 1981.

Poliakov, Leon, *Harvest of Hate: the Nazi Program for the Destruction of the Jews of Europe*, Philadelphia 1954.

Rotkowski, Adam, in *Le Monde Juif* Oct.-Dec. 1980.

Sauer, Paul, *Die Schicksale der Jüdische Burger Baden*, Stuttgart 1969.

Schramm, Hanna, *Vivre a Gurs*, Paris 1979.

Streib, Ludwig, *Die Israelitische Gemeinde in Hoffenheim, 1919-1945*, 1989.

Schwarzfuchs, Simon, *Aux Prises avec Vichy: Histoire Politique des Juifs de France, 1940-1944*, Paris 1998.

Walk, Joseph, ed., *Pinkhas Ha-Kehillot. Encyclopedia of Jewish Communities from their Foundation until after the Holocaust: Germany, Württemberg, Hohenzollern, Baden* (Hebrew) Jerusalem 1986.

Wiehn, E. G., *Oktober Deportation, 1940*, Konstanz 1990.

Ziegler, Karl, *Ortschronik Neidenstein*, Neidenstein 1962.

Zeitoun, Sabine, *L'Oeuvre de Secours aux Enfants (OSE) sous l'Occupation en France*, Paris 1990.

Archives

Archives de l'Alliance Israelite Universelle (AIU), Paris. Archives de l'Ecole Jules Ferry, Toulouse.

Archives de l'Oeuvre de Secours aux Enfants (OSE), Paris. Centre de Documentation Juive Contemporaine (CDJC), Paris.

Generallandesarchiv Karlsruhe (GLA).

Generalarchiv Stuttgart (STA).

Stadtarchiv Sinsheim (STA SNH).

Schweizerisches Bundesarchiv, Bern.

Schweizer Hilfswerk für Emigrantenkinder, Zurich.